General editor: Graham Handley MA Ph.D.

Brodie's Notes on George Eliot's
The Mill on the Floss

M
MACMILLAN

First published by James Brodie Ltd
Revised edition published 1977 by Pan Books Ltd

This revised edition published 1993 by
THE MACMILLAN PRESS LTD
Houndmills, Basingstoke, Hampshire RG21 2XS
and London
Companies and representatives
throughout the world

ISBN 0–333–58085–0

Typeset by Footnote Graphics, Warminster, Wiltshire
Printed in Great Britain by
Cox & Wyman Ltd, Reading

Contents

Preface

The intention throughout this study aid is to stimulate and guide, to encourage your involvement in the book, and to develop informed responses and a sure understanding of the main details.

Brodie's Notes provide a clear outline of the play or novel's plot, followed by act, scene, or chapter summaries and/or commentaries. These are designed to emphasize the most important literary and factual details. Poems, stories or non-fiction texts combine brief summary with critical commentary on individual aspects or common features of the genre being examined. Textual notes define what is difficult or obscure and emphasize literary qualities. Revision questions are set at appropriate points to test your ability to appreciate the prescribed book and to write accurately and relevantly about it.

In addition, each of these Notes includes a critical appreciation of the author's art. This covers such major elements as characterization, style, structure, setting and themes. Poems are examined technically – rhyme, rhythm, for instance. In fact, any important aspect of the prescribed work will be evaluated. The aim is to send you back to the text you are studying.

Each study aid concludes with a series of general questions which require a detailed knowledge of the book: some of these questions may invite comparison with other books, some will be suitable for coursework exercises, and some could be adapted to work you are doing on another book or books. Each study aid has been adapted to meet the needs of the current examination requirements. They provide a basic, individual and imaginative response to the work being studied, and it is hoped that they will stimulate you to acquire disciplined reading habits and critical fluency.

Graham Handley 1990

A close reading of the set book is the student's primary task. These notes will help to increase your understanding and appreciation of the book, and to stimulate *your own* thinking about it: *they are in no way intended as a substitute* for a thorough knowledge of the book.

The author and her work

'George Eliot', the pseudonym of Mary Anne Evans, later to call herself Marian Lewes, was born near Nuneaton in 1819. Her father was a land-agent who managed the estate of the Newdegate family, and Mary Anne, who early showed signs of precocious ability, had an older brother, Isaac, of whom she was very fond. Mary Anne acquired a solid grounding in modern languages as well as the classics and music, and as a young woman she was fervently evangelical. By 1842 she had grown away from a narrow concept of religion, and she became interested in German biblical criticism. This led to her translating Strauss's *Life of Jesus* (1846), though her name did not appear on the title page. By 1852 she had become assistant editor of the *Westminster Review*, a journal which surveyed a wide range of English and foreign literature from science and philosophy to contemporary poetry and fiction. She had made the acquaintance of George Henry Lewes, and gradually their relationship deepened. Lewes, actor, philosopher, biologist, critic, novelist, was a man of many parts; he was unhappily married, and he and Marian soon shared a warmth of sympathetic emotional and intellectual experience. In 1854 they determined to live together although they could not legally be man and wife; they went initially to Germany, and then returned to England, working hard at their writing, reviewing and, in Lewes's case, scientific studies. Just as the world of St Ogg's condemns Maggie, so Victorian morality condemned the Leweses, and Marian had a letter which she had written to her brother Isaac answered by his solicitor. Their few close friends stuck by them; theirs was a real marriage, a marriage of true minds and hearts, and it only ended with Lewes's death in 1878. Marian, alone and unable to be alone, turned for consolation to a close friend, John Walter Cross; he, twenty years her junior, had also been a friend of Lewes. Cross and Marian were married in 1880 but, after a honeymoon trip to Europe, Marian died in the December of that year.

The above is a skeletal outline of a remarkable woman and her even more remarkable story. Her life has always been the cynosure of attention; the apparent paradox of the woman who 'lived in sin' and yet wrote books of an unflinching personal morality has never ceased to fascinate both the eminent critic and the sensationalist intent on whetting the dubious appetite. Some of the titles stress the subjectivity of their authors: titles like *The True Story of George Eliot*, *The Inner Life of George Eliot*, *Marian*, *Marian Evans and George Eliot*, *George Eliot the Woman*. But today her reputation as a writer has out distanced biographical innuendo. It was in 1948 that F. R. Leavis published the most influential book of criticism of the English novel this century has so far seen; *The Great Tradition* established that the five major novelists were Jane Austen, George Eliot, Henry James, Joseph Conrad and D. H. Lawrence. Many years later Leavis was to acknowledge the greatness of Dickens, too, but the earlier book stimulated a series of critical investigations of the named writers which shows no sign of abating to this day. George Eliot has had at least her share of this attention, and the interested student will want to read the definitive and scholarly biography simply called *George Eliot* (1968) by Gordon S. Haight, as well as to look at Professor Haight's edition of *The George Eliot Letters* (Oxford, 1954–6) and perhaps Barbara Hardy's *The Novels of George Eliot* (Athlone Press, 1959).

There is nothing more absorbing than the account of how she came to write fiction; the entry in her journal for 6 December 1857 tells us how George Henry Lewes encouraged her, until

One morning as I was lying in bed, thinking what should be the subject of my first story, my thoughts merged themselves into a dreamy doze, and I imagined myself writing a story of which the title was – 'The Sad Fortunes of the Reverend Amos Barton'. I was soon wide awake again, and told G. He said, 'O what a capital title!' and from that time I had settled in my mind that this should be my first story. (*Letters* II, p.407)

And it was. 'The Sad Fortunes of the Reverend Amos Barton', the first of the *Scenes of Clerical Life*, was published in Blackwood's magazine, whither Lewes sent it from 'my clerical friend', and in February 1857 the pseudonym of 'George Eliot' was adopted; one remembers that Charlotte Brontë and her sisters had recourse to the same kind of masculine disguise, their works appearing under the names of Acton, Ellis and Currer Bell. 'Amos Barton' was followed in Blackwood's by 'Mr Gilfil's Love Story', while the final scene, 'Janet's Repentance', showed an uncompromising realism of treatment which was to characterize George Eliot's later work. Of her great contemporaries only Dickens was disposed to think that *Scenes of Clerical Life* had been written by a woman.

Marian was now launched on a writing career, but the tribulations of pseudo-anonymity were hard, particularly when an improvident clergyman, Joseph Liggins, claimed, and had claimed on his behalf, the authorship of the *Scenes of Clerical Life*. Meanwhile, Marian was hard at work on *Adam Bede*, which was published in 1859 and became one of the best sellers of the time. Her close friend, Barbara Bodichon, who had seen only extracts, was one of the few to penetrate the secret with an unerring certainty of identification and an equally direct honesty of delight:

1st. That a woman should write a wise and *humorous* book which should take a place by Thackeray.
2nd. That YOU *that you* whom they spit at should do it!
(*Letters* III, p.56)

The Liggins controversy reached the national press, and Marian was further distressed when an enterprising (and unscrupulous) publisher advertised a sequel, *Adam Bede Jnr*, which was, however, never published and probably never written. But, assisted by the indefatigable Lewes and the integrity of her publisher, John Blackwood, her unassailable position as author of both a literary and a popular success was established. She had already begun work on *The Mill on the Floss*, initially disagreeing with Blackwood about its publication, but later coming to advantageous terms with that most generous of publishers. After its publication (April 1860) she travelled to Italy with Lewes, who suggested that the life of Savonarola would make a good subject for a book. This idea was ultimately given a wider perspective in *Romola* (1863), but before that George Eliot determined to write another English story, *Silas Marner*, which was published in 1861. For the next two years she buried herself deep in research and writing ('She seems to be studying her subject as subject was never studied before', wrote John Blackwood); on its completion she was to write, 'great, great facts have struggled to find a voice through me'. *Romola* was not a great popular success, though it was published in the Cornhill Magazine as a serial, and Browning and Anthony Trollope both praised it.

Three years were to pass before another major novel was finished. *Felix Holt the Radical* (1866) marked her return to Blackwood's; it deals with English political and social life at the time of the first Reform Bill (1832) and contains a remarkable psychological portrait in the person of Mrs Transome, whose guilt and loneliness reflect a compelling realism. Marian's poem, 'The Spanish Gypsy', appeared in 1868, and then came her masterpiece, *Middlemarch*, which appeared in eight monthly parts in 1871–2. This 'study of provincial life', with its superb sense of structure, of inter-relationships, of imagery and moral awareness, sees her at the height of her intellectual and human power, at once ironic, compassionate, tolerant and wise. *Daniel Deronda* (1876), again issued in monthly parts like *Middlemarch*, is thought by many to be a splendid failure; to this writer it appears not so much a failure as a determined movement in another direction, in which the idea of Judaism is seen as the focal point of altruistic endeavour, of man's living for man in practical and spiritual integration. Although she was to complete *The Impressions of Theophrastus Such* (1878), her writing was effectively finished. Behind her, throughout the twenty-one years that spanned her output, stood George Henry Lewes, protective, reassuring, self-denying, giving himself to 'Polly', as he called her, unstintingly. As long ago as 1933 Anna Kitchel, in her *George Lewes and George Eliot*, indicated the nature of Marian's debt to Lewes; he continued to write himself but he was intent on Marian's fame, comfort and achievement rather than his own.

On what does George Eliot's reputation rest now? The answer must range widely if it is to do her justice. She brought to English fiction a high and serious purpose, a wide learning and culture, a scientific as well as a literary training. She recreated the nature of her childhood in unforgettable colours in her early writing, giving her books a historical authenticity, a 'local habitation and a name', and peopling them with a rich variety of humanity. And, like so many other writers, as she wrote an increasing intellectual awareness, a feeling for artistic organization, a sense that the completeness of real life could be rendered only by a like completeness of form – all these combined to give her novels perspective and authority. She revered Sir Walter Scott, and, like him she told a good story; her range extended from the dialect of rustics to the mannerisms of high society. She has been called the first modern novelist, and it is easy to see why. The literary technique known as 'the stream of consciousness' was not invented by Dorothy Richardson, James Joyce or Virginia Woolf; the exploration of consciousness and subconsciousness occurs throughout George Eliot's writings, and always with that degree of truth to experience, to the twistings and turnings of our fallible human nature which makes great literature real to us. Psychological immediacy, which makes us suffer with Maggie in her desolation, with Mrs Transome in her 'poor, lopped life,' with Adam Bede at Hetty's trial for child-murder, with Gwendolen on the 'plank-island' with Grandcourt – this is George Eliot's major achievement. And through her novels, perhaps she expiated in part those deep inner feelings of insecurity and guilt which were part of her nature; Frederick Myers has left us this account of her:

I remember how, at Cambridge, I walked with her once in the Fellows' Garden of Trinity, on an evening of rainy May; and she, stirred somewhat beyond her wont, and taking as her text the three words which have been used so often as the inspiring trumpet-call of men – the words God, Immortality, Duty – pronounced

with terrible earnestness how inconceivable was the first, how un-
believable the second, and yet how peremptory and absolute the
third. (*Essays: Modern*)

This sense of duty is the moral thread which runs throughout
her novels, binding her characters to put others before self;
but even when the dilemma or decision is not resolved, or is
wrong, or misguided, or culpable, the author's voice, compassionate but firm and wise, directs the reader's responses
towards the moral heart of the matter.

Plot summary

Background and chronology

Adam Bede was published on 1 February 1859, but Marian was soon at work on her next book, *The Mill on the Floss*. As early as 31 March she was writing to Blackwood about her new novel, but the advent of Liggins and the unwelcome publicity which he attracted inevitably caused her some concern. In June Blackwood read the first few chapters of the novel, which was provisionally called 'The Tullivers' or 'St Ogg's on the Floss' (later 'Sister Maggie' was considered), and was delighted with the tone and the treatment; perhaps he was also relieved, for he had published a story by George Eliot which was not to his liking – it was called 'The Lifted Veil' and ended with a particularly questionable blood transfusion. Marian was beset by her usual doubts, fearing that she would never again achieve the success of *Adam Bede*, though 'my stories grow in me like plants'. By September she was in Dorset with Lewes, looking at mills and gathering authentic material both for the setting of her novel and for its particular crisis of the flood.

Unfortunately, a coolness grew up between Marian and Blackwood over the terms of publication of the new novel, and it would seem that the fault lay with her. Nevertheless, she consulted Langford, Blackwood's London manager, about the legal problems of Tulliver's suit against Pivart in *The Mill on the Floss*. Meanwhile, she read Thomas à Kempis, and Dickens tried to obtain her services for his magazine *All the Year Round*. By December 1859 she and Blackwood were reconciled, and he read half the novel, saying of 'Sister Maggie' that it was 'a most wonderful portrait gallery and the humour and exquisite touches of nature make one pause upon every page'. In January 1860 he and Marian were debating the title; Lewes considered that 'Sister Maggie' sounded 'rather like a child's story'. Blackwood opted strongly for *The Mill on the*

Floss, and Marian accepted, though she observed that the Mill was on a tributary and she thought the title 'of rather laborious utterance'. But by 22 March she had finished the novel, the last eleven pages in a 'furore', and it was published on 4 April 1860.

It was an immediate and outstanding success. St Ogg's is generally to be equated with Gainsborough, but Marian researched mills and floods over a wide area before giving a precise setting to what is a strongly autobiographical narrative. According to Mudge and Sears, authors of *A George Eliot Dictionary* (1924), the great flood of the last chapter took place seventy years earlier (in 1770) than the one mentioned in the novel. But the overall chronology is clear. The opening finds the author looking back over thirty years (i.e. from 1859 to 1829) and, as always with George Eliot, historical references establish the time beyond doubt. Catholic emancipation and the burning of York Minster both belong to 1829, and Maggie is 'gone nine', the date of her birth being November 1819, the same as George Eliot's. The autobiographical element is more closely underlined when we note that Tom Tulliver was born in 1816 and is therefore almost the same age as Isaac Evans, George Eliot's brother, from whom she was estranged because of her liaison with Lewes.

When Tom returns to Mr Stelling's after the Christmas holidays (January 1830), he meets Philip Wakem, who is a year older than he is. Meanwhile Maggie goes off to school at Laceham, returning after her father's stroke (November 1832). The selling-up of the Tullivers' household effects takes place in the 'dark time of December', and in January (1833) Wakem buys the Mill. At the beginning of Book V we are told that Maggie is nearly seventeen and, a little later, that Philip is twenty-one. This effectively places the events in 1836, and the meetings of Maggie and Philip in the Red Deeps continue until Tom castigates Philip and exacts the terrible promise from Maggie that she will not see him again. This is in the spring of 1837, and shortly afterwards Mr Tulliver dies. Maggie is nineteen at the beginning of Book VI, and the date is June 1839 – Lucy being a year younger than Maggie. The following month Stephen and Maggie set out in the boat, go too far, are picked up by a Dutch ship and return to Mudport, where Bob Jakin sees Maggie who, exhausted and distraught, gets into the wrong coach and ends up in York. After her return to St Ogg's she stays with Bob, acts as governess to Dr Kenn's children, is visited by Lucy; and then the terrible rains begin as prelude to the flood which carries Tom and Maggie to their death. The Conclusion, the 'fifth' autumn after the flood, therefore belongs to 1844. Effectively the novel spans ten years, covering the period from Maggie's ninth to her nineteenth year.

Plot

Dorlcote Mill, home of the Tullivers, has been in the family for five generations. Maggie, aged nine, is devoted to her brother Tom, three years her senior, Mrs Tulliver is distinguished by having been a member of the Dodson family before her marriage, but her husband quick-tempered and fond of going to law, says that he married her because she was none too bright. Maggie is her father's favourite, but her mother constantly has to apologize for her to the Dodson aunts – Mrs Glegg, Mrs Pullet and Mrs Deane. The last-named has a blonde daughter a year younger than Maggie who is much closer than she is to the Dodson standard.

Tom is sent to school at Mr Stelling's, and is coached by that ambitious clergyman, who also takes as a pupil Lawyer Wakem's hunchbacked son, Philip. Mr Tulliver, it must be stressed, is in a state of constant bitterness against Wakem. Maggie visits Tom and meets Philip, and she is particularly grateful to Philip when the latter reassures Tom after he (Tom) has had an accident with a sword. Nevertheless the two boys do not get on, Tom being essentially unacademic and outdoor, while Philip is artistic and hypersensitive because of his disability. He adores Maggie.

Mr Tulliver, after another headstrong lawsuit, has a stroke, and Maggie is sent to fetch Tom home. The bailiffs are put into the Mill, and the Dodson aunts (and their husbands) hold a family council of lament and criticism which Maggie bitterly resents on her father's account; it is, however, instrumental in bringing out the family pride in Tom. He approaches Uncle Deane, and obtains a position in his firm, Guest and Company. Meanwhile Wakem, misguidedly approached by Mrs Tulliver, decides to buy the Mill and put Tulliver in as his manager; Tulliver accepts, but makes Tom swear undying enmity to the Wakems. Tom works hard to retrieve the family fortunes, Maggie begins to meet Philip regularly in the Red Deeps, reads Thomas à Kempis and learns the discipline of self-sacrifice. Philip loves Maggie, and Maggie feels a strong affection in return at this particularly drab time of her life.

When Tom learns of the friendship he humiliates Philip and forces Maggie to give up seeing him. With the aid of Bob Jakin Tom begins to trade on his own account, gets some money from Aunt Clegg, and succeeds in paying off his father's creditors well before either he or Mr Tulliver had considered it possible. But after the meeting Mr Tulliver assaults Wakem, and is only restrained by Maggie from severely injuring him; this brings on a stroke, and Tulliver dies. Maggie goes off to teach, and when we next meet her she has come back to visit her cousin Lucy. Maggie is now nineteen, beautiful and modest, and she greatly attracts Lucy's fiancé, Stephen Guest. He and Maggie fall in love, a fact which Philip notices, for he is frequently in their company and still loves Maggie himself. Lucy is unaware of this, and tries very hard to bring Philip and Maggie together, for she knows of their earlier meetings. Guest and Company buy back the Mill and Tom is established there as manager. Meanwhile, both Maggie and Stephen fight against their feelings, but when an opportunity occurs through the absence of Lucy and Philip they set off in a boat together. Maggie is unaware of the passage of time and distance, but she soon finds that it is too late to return. Stephen forces an admission of love from her, and almost persuades her to elope, but her strong sense of duty to others prevails, and when they are landed at Mudport by the Dutch vessel which has picked them up, Maggie determines to go back to St Ogg's.

Unfortunately she gets into the wrong coach and ends up in York. Later she returns to the Mill, where Tom treats her harshly and refuses to have anything to do with her. Her mother stands by her (as indeed does her Aunt Glegg) and Maggie finds lodgings with Bob Jakin. She works as a governess for Dr Kenn, but public opinion forces that good man (whose wife has died not long since) to give her up; Stephen and Philip write to her, and eventually Lucy, who has been made ill by the events, comes to Maggie and forgives her. Shortly after this there is heavy rain, the Floss rises to unprecedented levels, and Maggie rows to the Mill to warn Tom. The danger sweeps aside their differences, and they are once more as they were in childhood; but they in their turn are swept aside by the violence of the flood and the floating debris, and die clasping each other in the reconciliation which Maggie had longed for. The Conclusion carries the story forward another five years, with Philip occasionally visiting their grave alone and Stephen and Lucy, reconciled themselves, visiting it together.

Chapter summaries, critical commentary, textual notes and revision questions

Book First: Boy and girl

Chapter I: Outside Dorlcote Mill

The author says that she is watching the River Floss, on a day in February, as it flows towards the sea. On its banks stands the town of St Ogg's, a port to which many ships come sailing with cargoes of fir-planks, coal or seeds, valuable because of the oil they contain. Near St Ogg's the River Floss is joined by its tributary, the Ripple. The land around the river is farm land, and the whole area is divided into fields by flourishing hedgerows with many trees. Dorlcote Mill stands near a stone bridge across the river, and the sound made by the mill wheel, added to that of the water, is deafening. She also sees, in her imagination, a great waggon full of grain go over the bridge, and, nearer the mill, she sees a little girl who is apparently thinking so deeply that she takes no notice of her dog, which is trying to get her attention. The arms of the writer are numb with leaning on the bridge, she thinks – then, suddenly she realizes that she is in her own armchair and that she is resting heavily on its arms.

This effectively sets the scene for the whole novel, and raises narrative expectation through the promise of what is to come. The omniscient voice of the author is much in evidence, the description of the locale mature and confident. *The Mill on the Floss* is still considered by many critics to be fictionalized autobiography, and certainly the intimate tone here is a deliberate device to set the scene for a story. Notice the strong visual quality of the description.

broadening Floss The river is nearing its union with the sea.
fluted red roofs The roofs are covered with red tiles, which are arranged in grooves to carry away the rain water.
gables These are the upper triangular-shaped parts of the walls, with the ridge of the roof at the top.

transient glance Passing glance; the sun came out for a moment only.

beehive ricks The hay was piled in mounds or ricks that were rounded on top like a beehive.

withy plantation Collection of willow trees; these have flexible twigs which are used for binding things together.

bright-green powder Masses of microscopic plants form green patches on the damp side of tree trunks.

withes Twigs of the willow.

beaver bonnet Bonnet made from the fur of the beaver.

Chapter II. Mr Tulliver, of Dorlcote Mill, declares his resolution about Tom

Mr and Mrs Tulliver are discussing the education of their son Tom. Mr Tulliver wants him to have a good education and is not satisfied with the school which he is attending. Mrs Tulliver wants to consult her sisters and their husbands. Mr Tulliver, however, refuses to agree to this, but he promises that he will find a school near enough to the mill for Mrs Tulliver to do her son's washing and to send him some extra food. Mr Riley, the auctioneer, is coming next day, and Mr Tulliver decides to ask his advice about Tom's education. He would like Tom to become a professional man – a lawyer or doctor – but is afraid that he is not clever enough. Mrs Tulliver now begins to worry about her daughter Maggie, the little girl who was standing on the bridge. Maggie then comes in with her masses of black hair very untidy. She is a high-spirited, intelligent child, quite unlike the fair-haired, tidy, but rather dull, child of Mrs Tulliver's sister, Mrs Deane. Mrs Tulliver scolds Maggie about her untidy hair, and Mr Tulliver suggests that it should be cut off.

A wonderful scene of domestic interaction with Mr Tulliver in the ascendant and showing his obstinacy. A running humour informs the scene, with a fine control of dialect, and a clear definition of the different emphases for the man's world and the woman's. This sounds one of the themes of the novel. Maggie's entrance is typical: she is something of a natural rebel, this early appearance and her mother's horrified reaction showing that she is naturally unconventional, something that is brought out with compassionate irony as the plot unfolds.

as'll be bread to him i.e. which will enable him to earn a living.

th'academy George Eliot is trying to show Mr Tulliver's accent by spelling words as he would say them. The academy is the school Tom is attending at this time.

scholard Mr Tulliver's version of 'scholar'.

law suits and arbitrations Mr Tulliver was constantly disagreeing with his neighbours about the ownership of pieces of land, and in consequence he was often concerned in legal actions to claim what he considered to be his rights.

raskil Rascal.

vallyer Valuer.

no outlays . . . chain Some businesses cost nothing to set up; the watch chain is to impress possible clients.

fan-shaped cap Married women in those days covered their heads indoors as well as out; these caps were stiffened with starch and ironed so that their pleats stood out like a fan.

sanguinary Bloody; Mr Tulliver says that all the fowls may be slaughtered.

rhetoric He did not mean what he said; it was merely a figure of speech used for effect.

live independent i.e. they have enough money to live on without working.

wash him and mend him i.e. do his laundry and mend his clothes.

you can't step over it Mrs Tulliver imagines difficulties that do not exist.

i' summat In something (dialect).

Holland sheets These were made of fine unbleached linen of a brownish colour.

lay us out in The sheets were to be placed on the bed on which their bodies would lie after death, waiting for burial.

mangled Smoothed between the wooden rollers of a mangle.

lavender In those days linen was made to smell sweetly by having sprigs of lavender placed with it.

anticipating . . . sheets He might have thought that she was looking forward to the time when he would be dead.

tactile Known by touch; Mr Riley frequently touched his stockings.

false shirt fronts The men from the town, who speak as if they are very important people, are often careless; they wear a shirt until it is dirty, probably because they cannot afford another one, and then hide the dirt with a bib.

Bedlam creatur i.e. mad person. The name comes from the former Bethlehem Hospital in London, where lunatics were shut up.

mulatter Mulatto; child of a white person and a negro.

gell Girl.

patchwork Coverlets were made of small pieces of different kinds of material sewn together.

Madonnas Pictures of Mary, the mother of Jesus Christ.

Raphael A famous Italian painter (1483–1520). He lived at the time when the new ideas of the great surge of knowledge, known as the Renaissance, were bearing fruit. He did a great deal of work which may still be seen, especially in Rome.

Chapter III. Mr Riley gives his advice concerning a school for Tom

Mr Riley, the auctioneer, comes to visit Mr Tulliver on business, and as they are talking over their brandy and water, Maggie hears them mention her brother Tom, whom she adores. Mr Tulliver says that he does not want his son to be a farmer or a miller like himself, for he would then be waiting for his father's death in order to get his property. Maggie is indignant and protests, whereupon her father explains to Mr Riley what a clever child she is and Riley looks at the book she is reading; it is *The History of the Devil*, a very unsuitable book for a child. Mr Tulliver then asks about a school for Tom, and Mr Riley suggests that it would perhaps be better if the boy was sent to live at the house of a private tutor, and recommends the Rev Walter Stelling, a clergyman with a kind-hearted wife, who takes a few boys to educate.

Further evidence here of Maggie's independent spirit and of the main love of her life, her feelings for her brother Tom. Notice that education is something of a hit-and-miss business: already we can see George Eliot commenting ironically on the nature of the decision to be made, and we feel that it is a man's world. Maggie's cleverness is almost seen as something to be criticized, perhaps hardly tolerated. The running humour of the conversational exchanges continues.

cravat Wide cloth carefully arranged about the neck; it is the origin of the modern neck-tie.

appraiser Person licensed to decide the value of lands or goods for sale.

bonhommie Good-natured manner (Fr.).

his comb cut i.e. his pride humbled; the reference is to the comb of a cock.

Old Harry Name for the devil. Harry may be a corruption of 'hairy'; the Hebrew word 'scirium', meaning 'hairy', is translated as 'devils' in the Authorized Version of the Bible (Leviticus, XVII. 7).

rampant The term in heraldry for an animal represented standing upright on its hind legs.

Manichaeism The doctrine was introduced in the third century by Manes, who tried to combine Christianity with other religions. He believed that there were two Beings: Light (God) and Darkness (Evil or Satan), who was the author of all evil.

drive your waggon in a hurry i.e. act too quickly and without consideration.

Hotspur A character in Shakespeare's *King Henry IV, Part I*. He is an impetuous, fiery person, but a brave soldier; he is killed by the king's forces because he will not postpone the battle.

Skye terrier A kind of Scotch terrier with short legs and long hair; named from the Isle of Skye in the Western Isles, off the coast of Scotland.

pull my coat off before I go to bed i.e. never give up my authority while I am alive.

put off with spoon-meat ... teeth i.e. give my powers to younger men while I can still use them myself.

arms akimbo With hands on the hips and elbows held out.

petrifying wonder Mr Tulliver was so astonished that he seemed turned to stone.

Daniel Defoe English novelist and writer of pamphlets (1661–1731), who is best known for his novel *Robinson Crusoe*, the story of a man wrecked on a desert island; he also wrote *A Journal of the Plague Year* and *Captain Singleton*.

Jeremy Taylor's *Holy Living and Dying* Published in 1650 and intended to help people to lead good lives. Jeremy Taylor (1613–67) was a barber's son who became a great scholar and a bishop. He was Chaplain to King Charles I.

Aesop's Fables Aesop is supposed to have been a Greek slave set free by his master in the sixth century BC. The *Fables* are brief stories in which animals are the chief figures.

Pilgrim's Progress This book, published in 1678, was written by John Bunyan (1628–88), who was imprisoned for preaching. It is an allegory, a story with an underlying deeper meaning, describing the journey of Christian through the temptations of this life to the Celestial City.

Oxford man Member of the University of Oxford.

MA Master of Arts; this was Mr Stelling's degree.

never brew wi' ... Michaelmas day Mr Tulliver is teasing his wife, who is superstitious about the time for beginning a new venture; she is also anxious to keep her son at home as long as she can.

seven-leagued boots These are often mentioned in fairy stories; they are magic boots which enable the wearer to travel long distances in a short time.

For there is nothing ... imaginary game A man who is usually wise can be more wrong than a stupid man when he has the wrong idea, and anyone who believes that men always have a definite purpose for their actions is likely to be completely mistaken.

maladroit flatteries clumsy flatteries.

tincture of the Classics i.e. slight knowledge of Latin and Greek.

De Senectute A famous work on moral philosophy written in Latin by Marcus Tullius Cicero, the Roman lawgiver (106–43 BC). The title means 'On Old Age'.

Aenid Poem written by the Roman poet, Virgil (70–19 BC). It tells the story of the adventures of Aeneas, son-in-law of King Priam of Troy, after the city had been destroyed by the Greeks, and how he at last reached the shores of Italy.

Chapter IV. Tom is expected

Maggie is not allowed to go with her father to fetch Tom home from his boarding-school, so she soaks her hair with water in order that her mother may not try to curl it. Her mother is very cross, therefore Maggie goes up to the attic and gets rid of her bad temper by ill-treating her doll. Then she goes to the mill and talks with Luke, the head miller. She is horrified when he tells her that Tom's rabbits, which she had forgotten to feed, are dead. Luke invites her to pay a visit to his wife, and she does so.

This is one of the critical points of Maggie's young life (and there are many). The fetish represents the release for passionate feeling; just as important is her apprehension, fear of what Tom will say about her failure to feed the rabbits. Although this failure exemplifies the waywardness of Maggie's nature, we also feel for her because of the keenness of her suffering. With Tom's arrival now imminent, narrative expectation is aroused about his coming reaction.

gig Light carriage with two wheels drawn by one horse.

Fetish The Negroes of West Africa and other places believe that a stone, weapon or feather may be the abode of a spirit; if they possess the fetish they will have power over the spirit.

Jael destroying Sisera Jael was the wife of Heber, an Israelite, and Sisera was the defeated general of an enemy army. Sisera came to Jael's tent tired and hungry; she invited him in, and when he was asleep, she killed him by driving a tent-pin through his head (Judges, IV). For this she was praised as a heroine by her people (Judges, V. 24–27).

Pythoness In classical times she was the priestess of the god Apollo, and was supposed to be inspired by the vapours coming out of the ground at his temple at Delphi, in Greece. Many people came to consult the oracle and brought the priests rich presents.

auricula A kind of primrose.

au naturel In its natural state (Fr.).

enoo Enough.

civet cat An animal rather like a fox, which secretes a fluid that is used as a basis for making perfume.

corpses nailed to the stable wall Farmers and others nailed up the dead bodies of the destructive animals, which they had caught and killed, in an attempt to frighten away other animals.

gripe him Give him pain.

nash Weak.

lean-to pig sty This sty had been made by attaching a shed to the side of the cottage, using the outer wall of the cottage as the inside wall of the shed.

Sir Charles Grandison A novel by Samuel Richardson (1689–1761). Like Richardson's first novel, *Pamela*, it was in the form of letters, and was received with great enthusiasm.

Prodigal Son Reference to Jesus Christ's parable about the son who left his home and wasted his life and money until misfortune brought him back to his father's house, where his father welcomed him with delight although his elder brother was jealous. It symbolizes the forgiveness of God (Luke, XV. 11–32).

Chapter V. Tom comes home

When Tom and his father reach the mill, Mrs Tulliver and Maggie are waiting for them in great excitement. Tom has brought Maggie a new fishing-line, and she is very happy, until he suddenly decides to go and see his rabbits. She has to confess that they are dead, and he is so angry that she takes refuge in the attic – to weep. When teatime comes, she is missed by her parents and Tom is sent to find her. Brother and sister make up their quarrel, and next morning they spend a happy time fishing at the Round Pool.

That reaction is natural, Maggie's grief exacerbated as a result. Her dependence on him is now fully revealed. Brother and sister are here temporarily separated, as they are to be more definitely in adulthood later. Although Tom is not presented as sympathetically as Maggie, we feel some kinship for him at this stage. Notice how exactly George Eliot shows Mr Tulliver's power and his protective care of Maggie.

croft A field specially enclosed for keeping cattle.

generic character Character which he shared with all boys of his age.

cobnuts Hazel nuts.

leather Thrash.

tench A freshwater fish, like a carp.

Eagre A wave of great height which at certain times sweeps up the mouth of a tidal river.

Christiana The wife of the hero, Christian, in *Pilgrim's Progress* (see note p.23).

star flowers Wild anemones; pretty, white, English spring flowers.

speedwell Small, bright blue flowers which grow in English hedges; also known as bird's eye.

ground ivy Another wild plant, which has small, mauve flowers; it has no connection with the ordinary ivy.

Chapter VI. The aunts and uncles are coming

In Easter week, Mrs Tulliver decides to ask her sisters, Mrs Glegg, Mrs Pullet and Mrs Deane, to visit her. Mr Tulliver would like his own sister, Mrs Moss, and her husband to come too, but Mrs Tulliver objects. She is proud of being a member of the Dodson family, and she does not like her sister-in-law. On the day before the visit, Tom and Maggie discuss the food that is being prepared; they also discuss their cousin, Lucy Deane. Then they quarrel over a jam-tart. Tom is annoyed with Maggie and leaves her; she is miserable. Tom talks to Bob Jakin, the boy who is employed to frighten the birds away from the corn. They quarrel, too, and eventually fight because Bob will not give up a halfpenny which Tom wins from him.

The emphasis here is twofold – on the superiority of the Dodson half of the family on the one hand, and on natural childish quarrelling and interaction on the other. Family divisions, later to be seen in close-up, are here hinted at. The Tom–Bob Jakin relationship is also indicated. One can already see family friction developing.

cheese-cakes Small tarts made of curds, butter and sugar in a saucer-shaped pastry case.

I'd as lief not invite I would rather not invite.

'having' Greedy.

allays Always.

leggicy Legacy.

butter-money Most farmers' wives sold butter which they had made, and considered that the money from it belonged to them, not to their husbands.

It takes a big loaf ... breakfast When there are many people to share a fortune, the fortune must be large if each share is to be worth much.

hat bands In those days, each male mourner at a funeral wore a wide black band around his hat; it was considered a disgrace if these were not a real deep black.

small beer Very weak beer.

impedimenta Hindrances (Lat.).

bandy A kind of game played with a ball.

tipsy cake Sponge cake soaked in wine, stuck over with almonds and covered with custard or cream.

tomtit A kind of small bird, known also as a titmouse.

yellow-hammer A bird with yellow head, neck and breast.

stoats Small predatory animals, like weasels.

took her opium i.e. she used her imagination to make herself forget the troubles of the world, just as people who take opium drug themselves to forget.

rots Rats.

feyther Father.

ferrets Small animals kept for the purpose of driving rabbits or rats from their burrows so that they can be caught by dogs or men.

Noah's Ark When God destroyed most of mankind by a great flood, Noah was chosen to build a large boat or ark into which he was to take his own family and two (one male and one female) of every kind of creature. In this way the earth was re-peopled when the waters subsided (Genesis, VI–VIII).

heads and tails Game of throwing up a coin and guessing whether it will come down with the head of the monarch showing or the other side.

yeads Heads.

goldfinch A beautiful singing bird, with wings streaked with yellow and a red neck.

An' I'n gi'en And I have given.

curled fronts False hair to fasten across the front of the head.

tippet Narrow cape for the neck and shoulders; this one was made of fur.

chevaux-de-frise This really means a protective layer of hair on a plant, but here it means that Mrs Glegg wore a protection of frilling around her neck.

cravat See note p.22.

smack. A fishing vessel with only one mast.

brig A two-masted vessel.

Hottentot One of the original natives of South Africa.

buckram Coarse linen, very much stiffened.

a yard and a half across the shoulder The fashion was for exaggerated sleeves.

nevvy Nephew.

hare-skin on his chest This was intended to protect him from illness.

boluses Very large pills.

draughts He took very expensive medicine.

primeval strata She gave the oldest clothes she possessed.

Leghorn bonnet This was made of finely-plaited straw from Leghorn, in Italy.

musical snuff-box Most gentlemen carried a snuff-box and took a pinch of the powder every now and then; this box played a tune when opened.

'contrairy' Perverse, annoying.

tête-à-tête Quiet talk between two people (Fr.).

the keenness . . . contour i.e. you could find many men who had the same kind of figure, but not so many with the same intelligence in the eyes.

hinderlocks Hair at the back of Maggie's head.

Rhadamanthine Just, but stern. In classical mythology, Rhadamanthus was one of the three judges who decided what was to be the fate of each soul when, after death, it passed into the underworld.

Revision questions on Book First, Chapters I–VI

1 Give your first impressions of (a) Mrs Tulliver, (b) Tom Tulliver.

2 Describe Maggie Tulliver as she is when she first appears in the book.

3 What advice did Mr Riley give about Tom's education? What is your opinion of this advice?

4 Explain the meaning of Maggie's 'fetish'; how did it help her?

5 How did Mr Tulliver and his children react to the news that Mrs Tulliver intended asking her sisters and their husbands to visit her?

Chapter VII. Enter the aunts and uncles

Mrs Glegg arrives first at the Tullivers' house and gives advice to her sister about the meal she will soon be preparing for her guests, suggesting that she should not provide anything expensive. Presently, Mr and Mrs Pullet drive up. Mrs Pullet is in tears because a neighbour of hers has died of dropsy. Mrs Glegg thinks that this extravagant grief is ridiculous. Then Tom and Maggie come in from the garden; Maggie's hair is untidy, and she ignores her aunts and goes straight to her pretty little cousin, Lucy Deane, who has now arrived with her parents. Maggie is sent to have her hair brushed, but she is weary of being scolded about her hair, and, with Tom's assistance, she cuts it off. Immediately, she is frightened by what she has done and for a long time remains in her bedroom, refusing to go down to dinner. At last, however, she ventures to take her place at the table. Mrs Tulliver is horrified when she sees her, but Mr Tulliver takes Maggie's part and comforts her. When the children have been sent from the table, Mr Tulliver tells of his plan to send Tom to a clergyman to be educated. Mrs Glegg criticizes the plan, and they quarrel, whereupon Mrs Glegg leaves the house.

The sisters are seen in contrast, and the main characteristics of each are stressed. Note the bossiness of Mrs Glegg and the self-indulgent pathos of Mrs Pullet. There is a fine interplay of humour and a convincing use of dialect throughout. Maggie is of course unequal to the situation, but the cutting off of the hair underlines her impetuosity, something which is always present in her character. Again we see Mr Tulliver protecting his little wench. Mrs Glegg's power is abundantly demonstrated. The friction signalled in the previous chapter is now a fact.

thread-lace Lace made from linen or cotton threads.
he espoused it 'Espoused' means 'married'. Here it means that if he made a mistake he always tried to make it appear that it was something which had to happen and was not his fault.
Ajax When the Greeks besieged the city of Troy in order to recapture Helen, Ajax was the bravest soldier among them (see note on *Aeneid*, p.23).

blent Old form of 'blended'.

frock and trousers Small boys wore a kind of dress with long trousers underneath it.

half i.e. half of the school term.

which was felt to be so lacerating Which hurt so much.

burning glass A glass, a double convex lens, by which the sun's rays are focused on to dry wood to make it burn.

obfuscated Bewildered.

Lord Chancellor One of the most important people in England; he is the head of the legal system and Speaker of the House of Lords.

Old Harry See note p.22.

There's folks I've lent money to Mrs Glegg means Mr Tulliver.

causticity of tongue i.e. she had a bitterly sarcastic way of speaking.

Duke of Wellington Arthur Wellesley (1789–1852), the great British soldier whose skill in the Peninsular War helped to cause the abdication of Napoleon I of France; in 1815 he was mainly responsible for the defeat of Napoleon at the Battle of Waterloo.

Catholic Question This was whether the Catholics were to have freedom of action and worship in England, and caused a struggle between the political parties. The Duke of Wellington and Sir Robert Peel became convinced that they must be given freedom, and the Duke introduced a bill for this purpose into Parliament in 1829. He was accused of trying to bring back the power of the Pope in England and fought a duel in consequence.

Battle of Waterloo Fought in Belgium, near Brussels, on 18 June 1815. Napoleon's power was finally destroyed.

Blücher Field-marshal of Prussia (1742–1819); by arriving at Waterloo towards the end of the battle, he made Wellington's victory possible.

Dantzic A north European port belonging to Prussia in 19th century; a free city 1919–39; then German 'Danzig'; since 1945 Polish 'Gdansk'.

Papists Catholics, acknowledging the authority of the Pope.

Radicals Extremists who aim at fundamental changes in the methods of governing the country.

Chapter VIII. Mr Tulliver shows his weaker side

As a result of his quarrel with Mrs Glegg, Mr Tulliver determines to pay her the money she had lent him; however, he has not £500, so he determines to get back the money he has lent his sister's husband, Mr Moss. He therefore sets off for the home of Mr and Mrs Moss and their eight children, having made up his mind to be hard and stern. Mr Moss tells him that if the money has to be repaid he will be completely ruined. Mr Tulliver keeps his purpose, however, and rides away, leaving distress and sorrow behind him. Soon he begins to think of his children, Tom and Maggie, and this thought brings a new feeling for his own sister and a realization that he must help her. So he returns to her house and tells her he will manage without the money which her husband owes him.

Note the family likeness between Maggie and her father which this chapter reveals – Mr Tulliver's impetuous action means that, like Maggie, he suffers second thoughts. Family difference and the importance of money – the latter becoming increasingly vital as the plot unfolds – are seen in the contrast between the Moss family and their circumstances and the prosperous Dodsons we have seen in the previous chapter. Mr Tulliver's obstinacy is to lead to his downfall later on. Notice Aunt Moss and Mr Tulliver's feeling for her, a kind of Tom–Maggie adult situation deliberately echoed here.

patriarchal gold-fish This was a very old gold-fish, the grandfather of a large family, yet it had not learnt wisdom.
mortgaging Giving property to someone to whom you owe money as security that you will pay the debt; if you do not, he will keep your property.
dyspeptic Having indigestion.
promissory note A document containing a promise to do or not to do something: almost invariably used to promise repayment of a debt.
fallacious air Deceptive appearance.
plethoric Having too much blood.
too lofty . . . parchment His neighbours would borrow money but had no property which Mr Tulliver could seize if they failed to pay it back; so he had no legal document to protect him.
murrain An infectious disease among cattle; it is usually fatal.
fallow Land was allowed to lie fallow or to rest after it had been in cultivation for a time, to recover its fertility.

less than half a curate Basset shared a curate with several other
  parishes.
'Markis o' Granby' A reference to the village inn.
guttered candle The wax or tallow of the candle had melted
  irregularly.
as gates . . . known to do The gate swung against him.
Alsatia This was formerly a district in Whitefriars, London,
  where criminals and those who owed money could take refuge
  and the law could not touch them. The custom was abolished in
  1697.
didactic purpose She wanted to teach her children to love each
  other.
awk'arder More awkward, worse.

Chapter IX. To Garum Firs

Lucy Deane is staying with her cousins, Tom and Maggie,
and Mrs Tulliver takes the three children to see Mr and Mrs
Pullet. With much ceremony, Mrs Pullet takes her sister up-
stairs to show her her new bonnet. Maggie disgraces herself by
dropping the cake that Uncle Pullet has given her and then
stepping on it. Lucy then persuades him to let them hear his
musical snuff-box, and Maggie is so happy again that she
hugs Tom and makes him spill his drink. The children are
then sent outside to play while Mrs Pullet discusses her bad
health with her sister. Mrs Tulliver asks her to try and bring
about a reconciliation between Mrs Glegg and Mr Tulliver.
Just as the grown-ups are about to have tea, Sally, the maid,
opens the door to show an object which startles them all.

A further chapter of family interaction, with Maggie once
more responsible for the dissonance which occurs. George
Eliot delights in family interiors of this kind, and certainly her
ability to convey things from two perspectives, those of the
child and the adult, is demonstrated here. We expect crisis
and it comes fittingly at the end of the chapter.

Coronal locks His hair was cut to form a crown on the top of
  his head.
protective apparatus Apron or pinafore.
tuckers Part of a lady's dress, worn across the chest; they were

made of pieces of material which were tucked and adorned with lace.

pagoda A Buddhist temple built in the form of a pyramid.

circumstantial evidence Maggie did not want to destroy what Tom had built, but the circumstances seemed to show that she acted deliberately.

superannuated bluebottle i.e. elderly fly, old enough to be given a pension.

Cousin Abbot may go i.e. she may die.

fly-cages These contained a sticky substance to trap flies.

Aristotle Famous Greek philosopher (384–322 BC); he was trained as a physician, and his works are scientific in many ways. The chief are *Physics, Politics, Ethics* and *Poetics*.

miniatory Threatening.

cockchafers Maybugs, large insects that make a humming sound and can sting.

Ulysses and Nausicaa When Ulysses, the Greek hero, was on his way home after the city of Troy had been captured and burnt, he had many adventures and suffered many hardships. On one occasion, after being shipwrecked, he was washed up on the shores of the king of the Phaeaceans, where the king's daughter, Nausicaa, saw him as she was playing with her friends. She and her father both helped him, and later she married the son of Ulysses.

lives too low i.e. is too frugal.

Turkey rhubarb Root of a plant obtained from China, in spite of its name, and used as a medicine.

Ladyday 25 March, the day of the Church's festival of the Annunciation of the Virgin Mary, the time when the Angel told her that she was to have a son, Jesus.

damask napkin Fine table linen.

Chapter X. Maggie behaves worse than she expected

The object brought by Sally to the door is little Lucy, completely covered in mud. When the children were sent out to play, Tom was displeased with Maggie because she had made him spill his cowslip wine, so he was very attentive to Lucy and presently persuaded her to go to the pool and look at the great fish, a pike, which lived there. This was against orders, for they had been forbidden to leave the garden. Tom made Lucy stand on a patch of grass so that she would not get her feet dirty. However, Maggie, who was exceedingly jealous of Lucy because Tom was taking notice of her, followed them and pushed Lucy into the mud. Tom brought her back to the house and handed her over to the maid, explaining what Maggie had done. It is now discovered that Maggie has disappeared. Tom suggests that she has gone home. So her mother and brother set off to find her.

Another demonstration of Maggie's impetuosity and of her possessiveness over Tom, the latter being the dominating factor in her early life. But there is tension aroused too over her disappearance, and the narrative is beginning to flow easily.

unprecedented apparition i.e. such a sight had never been seen there before.

Medusa One of the three Gorgons; her hair was of snakes and she could turn into stone anyone who looked at her. Perseus cut off her head while he watched her reflection in the shield which the goddess Athene had given him, since he dare not look directly at her.

insurrectionary visit They had been forbidden to go to the pond, so it would be insurrection or rebellion to go.

sultan Title of a Mohammedan ruler, especially of the Ottoman Empire. He was always a tyrant with supreme power.

corpus delicti This Latin phrase is a legal term meaning the foundation or body on which the wrongdoing is based. Here George Eliot is making a joke – that the body in this case is the muddy Lucy.

ignominious manner i.e. in a way to make them feel ashamed.

horse-block A large block of stone or wood on which people stood to mount a horse.

I wish . . . enough Mrs Tulliver wishes that the River Floss was farther away, as she is afraid that her children may get drowned. Her words foreshadow what will happen later.

revolutionary aspect Mr Pullet's orderly life had been upset by Maggie as if by a revolution.

Chapter XI. *Maggie tries to run away from her shadow*

Maggie has run away to find the gipsies. She meets two shabby-looking men to whom she gives a sixpenny piece. She is looking for Dunlow Common, and at last, tired and hungry, she comes to what is obviously a gipsy encampment. A young woman with a baby speaks to her with great respect, and Maggie is delighted, because she feels that the gipsies realize how superior to them she is, and she hopes that they will make her their queen. The gipsies take her bonnet and one of the girls makes fun of her. She asks for food and they give her bread and bacon, which she does not like. They talk in a language she cannot understand and their manners are rough, so that she decides she cannot be their queen. Presently, they enquire where she lives, and one of the men puts her before him on a donkey to take her home. On the way they meet Mr Tulliver and there is a joyful reunion. Maggie promises never to run away again.

The whole chapter is symbolic of Maggie's frustration and her (temporary) wish to escape into another world where she is a person of importance. It also signals an outside world of reality, sordid reality, about which Maggie is completely ignorant. George Eliot balances this experience neatly between comedy and a certain fear. Maggie's perspective, her essential naiveté, is well conveyed.

gypsies A race of wandering, dark-skinned people, probably of Hindu origin, known in all European countries; now more usually spelt 'gipsies'.

in harmony with circumstances i.e. enjoying the kind of life which would suit her.

the idea of parting . . . very much Maggie's only regret was leaving her father.

passengers Passers-by.

common. Common land originally belonged to a whole village, and on it any villager was allowed to keep his animals in the days before the Enclosure Acts.

half past four by the sun Aunt Pullet's clock was half an hour fast.

a log to his foot He was tethered to a log to prevent him from straying.

Apollyon A fiend which attacked Christian in Bunyan's *Pilgrim's Progress*.

diabolical blacksmith He is the one pictured in Maggie's copy of *The History of the Devil*.

fungus A growth, like a mushroom, which never becomes green.

blighting obloquy Reproaches which were spoiling her life.

skewer A piece of wood which had been smoothed so that it could be stuck through food for cooking – like a sharpened pencil.

sphinxes The children were as motionless and had as little change of expression as the Sphinxes in Egypt.

a language which Maggie . . . understand The gipsies have their own language, known as Romany.

hindforemost The girl put the bonnet on back to front.

Columbus Christopher Columbus (1451–1506) was an Italian from Genoa, who was given help by King Ferdinand and Queen Isabella of Spain to set out on a voyage of discovery. He thought he would be able to sail round the world westwards to India, but instead he discovered the New World of the Americas in 1492.

Catechism of Geography A book which gave questions and answers about the geography of the world.

platters Flat dishes made of wood.

treble sauciness The three women all answered the man in an impudent way.

Robin Hood Hero of a large number of old English ballads, in which he is shown as a gallant and generous outlaw living in Sherwood Forest with his merry men, among them Friar Tuck and Little John, and with his wife, Maid Marion. He robbed the rich to help the poor. The stories are supposed to have been founded on a real person, the Earl of Huntingdon, who became an outlaw in the time of Richard I when Prince John, afterwards the infamous King John, was ruling England for his brother.

Jack the Giantkiller A character in many old stories, he had incredible adventures and defeated many giants by cunning means.

Mr Greatheart Another character from Bunyan's *Pilgrim's Progress*; he was the heroic escort who guided Christiana and her children to the Celestial City.

St George Patron Saint of England; the story says that he defeated and killed a terrible dragon.

Leonore She appears in a poem of the same name by Edgar
Allan Poe; he describes her as a 'rare and radiant maiden'.

Chapter XII. Mr and Mrs Glegg at home

The history of the town of St Ogg's is given, with the legend
of Ogg, the ferryman, who in early times had conveyed
travellers across the River Floss. One stormy night, according
to the story, a woman and a child came to the river; the other
boatmen refused to take them across but Ogg did as they
wished. When they reached the other bank the woman revealed herself as the Virgin Mary; the child in her arms was
Jesus Christ. When Ogg died, his boat drifted out to sea and,
later, it was believed that when the river was in flood this boat
was to be seen on the waters with Ogg rowing and with the
Virgin in the prow. Mr and Mrs Glegg live in St Ogg's. One
morning at breakfast, soon after the visit to the Tullivers when
Mrs Glegg had quarrelled with her brother-in-law, Mrs Glegg
is angry with her husband because he disapproves of the way
she behaved and of her plan to recall the money which she had
lent Mr Tulliver. All day she continues to show her anger by
reading a book of meditations on religion, but in the evening
husband and wife talk to each other normally again.

This is another finely balanced chapter, the St Ogg's legend
being of major importance in the structure of the novel since,
much later, Maggie too is to be the Virgin of St Ogg's, though
not thought so by the world and his wife. The movement from
legend to reality is here ironically made. George Eliot is adept
at portraying marriage, and here we have the name and
nature of Mr and Mrs Glegg spelled out. Each reads the other
well, and Mrs Glegg, despite her domineering nature, knows
exactly when to come down into reasonable reality from her
sulk. This is another chapter which demonstrates the quality
of George Eliot's humour.

red-fluted See note on 'fluted red roofs', p.18.
unlade Unship, unload.
classic pastorals Many of the early classical poets wrote of
people as shepherds and shepherdesses. But they did not show

the lives of country people as they really were – they made everything pleasant and attractive at all times.

bower-birds The name given to several kinds of Australian birds which make elaborate nests.

white ants These creatures make wonderful homes, with long passages inside a mound which they have constructed.

millennial tree Tree which has lived for a thousand years.

Roman legions The Romans captured Britain and occupied it for over four hundred years; they left in AD 411.

sea-kings These were the Danes who came on marauding expeditions and then began to settle in the country. Danish kings ruled England from 1017 to 1040.

Saxon hero-king Alfred the Great (840–90). He defeated the Danes and then made peace with them.

tumulus A mound made over a grave in early times.

Normans The Northmen who settled in northern France. William, Duke of Normandy, won the Battle of Hastings in 1066 and became king of England; he is known as William the Conqueror.

oriel A large recess containing a window, which projects from the upper part of a house.

Gothic façade A front made in Gothic style. Gothic architecture has high, pointed arches and clusters of pillars.

trefoil ornament i.e. in the form of a leaf, like a clover leaf, with three segments.

half-timbered Built partly of wood. Old houses often have the upper part half timber and half plaster in strips.

hagiographer Person who writes the lives of saints.

Blessed Virgin The Mother of Christ (see note on 'Ladyday', p.33).

Civil Wars These took place in the seventeenth century, when the Parliament of England and its supporters rose against King Charles I and his friends; the wars ended with the execution of the king and the setting up of a Commonwealth under Oliver Cromwell. In 1660, however, the monarchy was restored under Charles I's son, Charles II.

Puritans Protestants of the seventeenth century who were very narrow in their beliefs and strict in their lives.

Loyalists Usually known as Royalists; supporters of Charles I.

stucco-facing Coating of the fine cement placed over the bricks making a wall.

Russia . . . came from. Linseed is made from the seeds of the flax plant and could be obtained in large quantities only from Russia.

grist Corn for grinding. There is an old proverb, 'To add grist to the mill', meaning to increase an already abundant supply.

The Catholics . . . trade Superstitious people blamed these three causes for all the misfortunes of men.

John Wesley (1708–91) At first he was a clergyman of the Church of England, but in 1738 he became convinced, quite suddenly, that Christ had swept away his sins. As a result, many of his fellow clergymen forbade him to preach in their churches and he founded a sect, the Methodists or Wesleyans, which has become stronger and stronger from that time on.

Dissenting pulpits Those who believed in the new ideas and did not agree with the Church of England were known as Dissenters.

chandlering Selling candles and similar goods.

Catholic Question See note p.30.

Independent minister He belonged to another sect of those who did not follow the teachings of the Church of England and called themselves Independents or Congregationalists.

wool-stapler Dealer in wool.

But it is well known . . . kind Wives who approved of the things in which their husbands found pleasure were considered weak by Mrs Glegg, for they did not seem to realize that a wife ought to prevent her husband from having any pleasure at all, since his hobbies were certain to be unreasonable.

man's rib Allusion to the creation of Eve from Adam's rib (Genesis, II. 22).

zoological phenomena Strange happenings in the animal world.

York Minster Famous cathedral of York. It is the cathedral of the Archbishop of York.

lovable skinflint One who hoards his money and refuses to spend it, but who is, nevertheless, attractive.

cheese parings Rind cut from cheese; misers were said to be unwilling to throw away even these.

turnpike Bar placed across a road to prevent coaches or foot passengers from continuing their journey until they had paid toll.

inalienable habit i.e. habit which had become so much a part of his character that he could not break it.

harrier A kind of dog used for hunting hares.

Harpagon Name of the miser who is the chief character in the play *L'Avare*, by the French dramatist Molière (1622–73).

too pungent seasoning Mrs Glegg's good points had been strongly exaggerated when he married her, for she was not young and was set in her ways.

less leathery consistence Mrs Glegg's pastry was not good, but Mr Glegg had got into the habit of thinking it right to make pastry in that way.

state of cavil State of being peevish and objecting to everything he said.

cut off with a shilling When a father disapproved of the actions of a son or daughter, he might leave a will mentioning his disapproval and leaving the offender only one shilling of his money.

fuzzy curled front Mrs Glegg had several 'fronts' of false hair; she wore this one only when she was ready to receive visitors (see note on 'curled fronts', p.27).

as meek as Moses Moses, the leader of the Israelites in the wilderness, submitted meekly to the will of God (Exodus).

gruel Invalid food, thin porridge made from oatmeal.

Baxter's *Saints' Everlasting Rest*. A famous work dealing with the way to live a good life. Richard Baxter (1615–91) was a Puritan who lived during the Civil War (see note p.38). He was badly treated in the reign of James II because he joined the Duke of Monmouth's rebellion in 1685. Monmouth claimed the throne, and Baxter believed that if James could be driven out, the country would be safe from the Catholic regime.

parenthetic hint Mr Glegg had hinted quite casually that if he died his wife would be well cared for.

weeper Widows and other mourners wore long black ribbons on their hats; these were known as weepers, and the length was supposed to indicate the amount of sorrow they felt (see note on 'hat bands', p.27).

testamentary tenderness He expressed his fondness for her by leaving her a large fortune.

eulogistically Praising him greatly.

banks . . . pleasure of property i.e. she would like to keep her money hidden at home where she could see and count it.

food in capsules This sounds very modern. Mrs Glegg ate for pleasure and not merely to keep alive.

Chapter XIII. Mr Tulliver further entangles the skein of life

Mrs Pullet visits Aunt Glegg in order to try and end the quarrel between Mrs Glegg and Mr Tulliver; she finds her task easier than she expected, and Mrs Glegg declares that everything is to be as in the past. However, Mr Tulliver has already written to Mrs Glegg saying that he is going to return her money and, although she is welcome to visit his house, he desires no favours from her, either for himself or his children. The letter has been written because Mrs Tulliver has told him about Mrs Pullet's visit to Aunt Glegg to persuade her to forgive him; he is very indignant. The ill-feeling between Mrs Glegg and her brother-in-law is increased, and when Mrs Glegg next visits her sister she does not enter the house. Mr Tulliver does not find it easy to borrow the money to pay Mrs Glegg, and at last has to get it from a client of Lawyer Wakem.

Mr Tulliver's obstinacy and pride are exemplified in this chapter. George Eliot is here subtly emphasizing the nature of human motives and interactions: there is a might-have-been quality about the whole thing which is true to our own life experiences. Reconciliation is so near and yet, because of the nature of the main personalities involved, so far.

piqued his pride Made him feel that he had been humbled.

the relation . . . puzzling world Mr Tulliver finds it difficult to write a letter because he cannot spell.

not make your legacies . . . degrees of kinship In her will she had divided her money between her relatives so that those more nearly related to her had more money than those who were only distantly connected.

the salt of our provincial society The strict fairness and honesty with which the people in provincial towns behaved kept the standards of the whole country at a high level.

Oedipus King of Thebes, whose story is told in a play by the Greek dramatist Sophocles. He did not know his parents and unwittingly killed his father and married his own mother. When the truth was revealed to him, he put out his eyes and left Thebes.

Revision questions on Book First, Chapters VII–XIII

1 Write short character-sketches of Maggie's four aunts: Mrs Glegg, Mrs Deane, Mrs Pullet and Mrs Moss. Which one do you like best? Give your reasons.
2 What do you learn about Maggie from her behaviour when Mrs Tulliver, her children and her niece visited Aunt Glegg?
3 Chapter XIII has a heading – 'Mr Tulliver further entangles the skein of life'. Explain exactly how he does this.
4 When and in what way are the following mentioned in these chapters: Mr Greatheart, Oedipus, Harpagon, Hottentot, Blücher? Write a brief note on each.
5 Why did Maggie run away to the gipsies? What happened to her and why did she leave them?

Book Second. School-time

Chapter I. Tom's 'first half'

Tom's first half-term with the Rev Mr Stelling is described. He finds the master stern and difficult to understand, for Mr Stelling is a very ambitious man and, as he has heard that he may get another pupil from the same district as Tom, he wishes to make Tom show some improvement in his work. Tom finds the life at the vicarage lonely with no one of his own age to play with. Mrs Stelling's second baby is born and Tom has to look after her little daughter, Laura. When Mr Tulliver comes to visit his son, he brings Maggie with him. She stays for a fortnight and tries to understand Tom's lessons. When she goes he misses her greatly, but at last the Christmas holidays come round.

The switch to Tom and his mis-education is effectively done. George Eliot's irony plays over the fact of Mr Stelling's ambition and also his inability to understand a boy like Tom. I said 'mis-education' above because Tom does not need the rote-learning classical instruction which Mr Stelling provides.

We are moved to pity for him: after Maggie's visit we are aware of the depths of *his* deprivation.

copperplate A kind of writing that was very neat with each letter carefully formed: it takes its name from the polished copper plate on which words were engraved for printing.

arabesques Ornamentation in the style of Arabic art. Some people in those days surrounded their signatures with an elaborate design of fine lines.

'My name is Norval' A quotation from a play called *Douglas* by John Home (1724–1808), often used as a passage for children to recite.

Gospel and Epistle Parts of the Communion service of the Church of England.

Collect A special prayer for each day contained in the Book of Common Prayer, the service book of the Church of England.

percussion-caps Small copper caps containing explosive powder, as used in a toy revolver.

inclining to brazenness Rather bold.

Massillon. A famous French preacher (1663–1742) who preached before Louis XIV and Louis XV; his sermons show great power, and Mr Stelling had learnt parts of them by heart.

Bourdaloue Another French preacher (1632–1704); he was sent to persuade the Protestants to become members of the Catholic Church again, after their rights had been taken from them.

evangelicalism. Low Church doctrine; faith should be based upon the principles laid down in the four Gospels.

Lord Chancellor See note p.30.

procrastination of the fruits of success Wasting time in planning what success would bring him.

new readings Many of the plays have single words or whole passages missing, and the scholars who edit them try to supply the words.

decline Give the grammatical forms of a noun.

pun Mr Stelling uses the word in its two meanings: 'to give the grammatical cases' and 'to refuse'.

maltster Maker of malt for beer.

sessions Court of Petty Sessions where minor cases are tried.

'swing' Enthusiasm, fervour.

second confinement Mrs Stelling's second baby was born.

monthly nurse Nurse who attended the mother and stayed for a month to look after her.

Binny This was the name of the beaver.

Eton Grammar The famous Latin Grammar book used at Eton College, the English public school.

Euclid The Greek scholar who taught in Alexandria about 300 BC, and whose book *Elements* is the best-known early book on mathematics and that on which modern geometry is based.

Aristotle Greek philosopher (384–322 BC) who established a school of rhetoric at Athens.

deaneries and prebends Offices in the Church of England.

'mapping and summing' Mr Tulliver wanted Tom to know how to draw maps and to learn the names on them and to do sums.

the relations between cases and terminations In Latin, the various cases of a noun have different endings. The genitive is the possessive case, i.e. Latin 'mensae' means 'of a table'; the dative is the case of the indirect object, i.e. Latin 'mensis' means 'to or for tables'.

pointer from a setter Kinds of dogs trained to deal with game. The pointer indicates or points the game by pointing his muzzle towards it as he sniffs, whilst the setter remains rigid when game is found.

regimen Rule.

Delectus A book containing a collection of passages for translation, especially from Latin and Greek.

shrew-mouse . . . cattle Superstitious country men used to split a tree and imprison therein a small animal, believing that this would remove bad luck that caused illness in cattle.

nodus Knotty point or difficulty (Lat.).

calenture Violent fever.

peccavi I have sinned (Lat.).

syntax Construction of a sentence and the arrangement of words.

Mors omnibus est communis Death is common to all (Lat.).

Appellativa arborum The naming of trees (Lat.).

sunt etiam volucrum There are also birds (Lat.).

Ceu passer, hirundo Like the sparrow and swallow (Lat.).

Ferarum Of wild beasts (Lat.).

tigris With tigers (Lat.).

vulpes Foxes (Lat.).

et Piscium And of fish (Lat.).

mascula nomia in a Masculine nouns in a. Maggie is hearing the grammar which Tom has to learn.

nomen non creskens genitivo Tom is now making fun of his sister's pronunciation of the Latin phrase.

limbo The place where the souls of those good people who died before the birth of Christ were supposed to abide.

cistus Latin name of the rock rose.

fuchsia An attractive shrub with long bell-like flowers.

Chapter II. The Christmas holidays

Tom comes home for Christmas, but although Maggie and he decorate the house as usual, he feels that there is something wrong. His father is more irritable than usual; the reason for this is that he is engaged in a quarrel with a Mr Pivart, who is taking water from the river above Dorlcote Mill in order to irrigate his land. There is thus less water power for the mill. Mrs Moss and Mrs Tulliver try to persuade him not to go to law. When Tom is about to return to Mr Stelling's house, he hears that the son of Lawyer Wakem is also to go there as a pupil.

This is a fine atmospheric chapter, with some telling seasonal description, but the main effect is of the adult fear which communicates itself to the children. Mr Tulliver's obstinate and aggressive nature becomes more evident. Narrative interest is again aroused by the news of Lawyer Wakem's son going to Stelling.

neatliest Most neatly arranged.

dyspeptic Puritans The Puritans disapproved of many things which other people found pleasurable, including feasting at Christmas-time, and George Eliot suggests that they suffered from indigestion.

damson cheese A favourite dish.

a priori ground The Latin phrase means 'from the former', and a person is said to argue *a priori* when he assumes that because a certain action is the right thing to do it will be done. Mr Moss believed that because Mr Tulliver was his brother-in-law he must support him.

dykes Banks built to send the water across Mr Pivart's fields.

erigations Irrigations.

strongest spurs In the barbarous sport of cock-fighting, metal
spurs were fastened to the claws of the birds.

nuts to Old Harry i.e. the devil has had great pleasure from
this.

collateral Related, although in a parallel line of the family and
not directly.

right of road It there has been a path across of piece of land for
many years, a right of way is established in law and the path
cannot normally be closed.

his weakness . . . scrupulosity He would not lose money by
being too honest.

irrefragable Unanswerable.

Chapter III. The new schoolfellow

At last Tom has to return to his studies with Mr Stelling. He
takes with him presents for Laura, Mr Stelling's little girl.
When he arrives, Mr Stelling sends him into the study to meet
Philip Wakem, who is to study with him. Philip is the son
of Lawyer Wakem, whom Mr Tulliver dislikes, so Tom is
prejudiced against him, his prejudice being increased by the
fact that Philip is hunch-backed due to an injury when he was
a baby. When Tom meets Philip he finds that not only can he
draw well, but also that he knows a great number of exciting
stories, some about the Greeks and others about the Scots.
The two boys talk to each other, and as they are called to
dinner Tom decides that Philip has a disagreeable side to his
character.

This firmly establishes the major differences between Tom
and Philip – they are certainly physical and also emotional
and mental. Notice how George Eliot conveys Philip's sensitivity through his deformity, and Tom's prejudices through
his father's attitude to Lawyer Wakem. It is ironic that Mr
Stelling's education should, in so many ways, be suitable for
Philip: and note the latter's talent and imagination.

Dutch doll This would be made of wood, with a round face that
had two patches of red painted on the cheeks, and black hair.

gig-umbrella A large umbrella placed over an open vehicle.

comforter Scarf.

physiognomist One who judges character from the study of faces.

not a congenital hump i.e. Philip had not been born with a deformed back, he had had an accident when a baby.

Propria quae maribus Section of the Latin Grammar.

epigrammatic intention He did not intend to make a witty remark.

Socrates Most celebrated philosopher of ancient Greece. In 399 BC, at Athens, he was charged with neglecting the gods of the state and was condemned to death. He spend his last day chatting with friends and then drank hemlock.

David and Goliath David was the shepherd boy who killed the giant Goliath, champion of the Philistines, by the use of his sling and a smooth pebble (I Samuel, XVII).

Samson An Israelite famous for his great strength, which was supposed to depend upon his hair. His wife, Delilah, discovered this, cut off his hair, and betrayed him to the Philistines, the enemies of the Jews; they blinded him. In his captivity his strength returned as his hair grew, and he pulled down the temple of their god, killing himself and a host of his enemies (Judges, XVI).

Odyssey The great epic poem by Homer, in which he describes the adventures of Ulysses or Odysseus, the Greek hero, after the capture of Troy.

Polypheme King of the Cyclops; a race of monsters who had only one eye, placed in the middle of their foreheads. Ulysses and his sailors were captured by him when they landed on his shores, and escaped with great difficulty after Ulysses had played a trick on him.

Richard Coeur-de-Lion and Saladin Richard I of England, known as the Lion-heart (1157–99), went on a Crusade to rescue the Holy Land from the Turks, whose leader was the chivalrous Saladin (1137–93), Sultan of Egypt. Richard defeated Saladin at Caesarea and at Jaffa.

William Wallace and Robert Bruce William Wallace was the Scottish patriot who fought against Edward I of England. He was defeated in battle at Falkirk, and condemned and executed by the English in 1305. Robert Bruce was the hero of the Scottish war of independence against Edward I of England. He defeated Edward II at the battle of Bannockburn (1314).

James Douglas There were several figures of Scottish history belonging to the Douglas family called James. One of them fought against James II of Scotland and had to escape to England. Another, the Black Douglas, fought with Wallace.

Chapter IV. The young idea

Tom's education is described. Mr Stelling is not a good schoolmaster, because he knows nothing of education. However, although Tom is not a good scholar, he improves, largely owing to Mr Poulter, the village schoolmaster, an old soldier. One day Tom persuades Mr Poulter to bring his sword to show him, and later gives Mr Poulter five shillings to allow him to keep the sword for a few days. Tom tries to persuade Philip to watch Mr Poulter's exhibition of swordsmanship, and this hurts the unfortunate boy who, because of his deformity, cannot perform any physical exercises. They quarrel, and Tom says that Philip's father is a rogue.

Mr Stelling's lack of understanding is fully revealed, and the distance between Tom and Philip matches that of their parents. Tom is a natural boy, Philip hasn't the health or the physique to be so. So many of George Eliot's effects are achieved through contrast, which is exemplified here.

mere perception predominates . . . emotion Tom was the kind of boy who judged everyone by appearances and first impressions, instead of thinking deeply.

Saladin See note p.47.

Robert Bruce See note p.47.

Bannockburn See note on 'William Wallace and Robert Bruce', p.47.

the top of his bent As much as he was capable of; the phrase is taken from Shakespeare's *Hamlet*, III. ii.

no faculty to spare i.e. he had no wish to learn the art of teaching.

impromptu . . . phonetic fashion They spelt words as they sounded, or invented a spelling as they went along.

circular A bill sent round to advertise some event, commodity or place; here it was a school.

some ambitious draper These men, who knew nothing of education, would imitate the mistakes of other parents.

a ripe scholar . . . market The masters in charge of these schools were allowed to keep their posts after they became too old for them.

thumb-screw An instrument of torture used in the Middle Ages.

Virgil The greatest of the Latin poets (70–19 BC), who wrote the *Georgics*, the *Eclogues* and the long epic poem, the *Aeneid*, which tells how the Trojan hero Aeneas came to Italy and founded Rome (see note p.23).

divinae particulum aurae A ray of divine light (Lat.). A quotation from the Latin writer Lucretius.

Theodore Hook's novels Hook (1788–1841) is best known as a writer of operas and as editor of a periodical, *John Bull*; however, he wrote nine novels.

promiscuous education Education obtained haphazardly and more or less by chance.

Peninsular soldier He had served under the Duke of Wellington in the war against Napoleon Bonaparte, French emperor from 1798 to 1814. The peninsula consists of Spain and Portugal.

superannuated charger An old war horse which has been pensioned off.

Hector A son of Priam, King of Troy, and the greatest of the Trojans; he was killed by Achilles.

Achilles The greatest of the Greeks; he was the hero of Homer's epic poem, *The Iliad*.

Bony Nickname given to Napoleon Bonaparte.

Talavera A town in Spain where Wellesley (later Wellington) defeated the French in the Peninsular War (1809).

Siege of Badajos An incident of the Peninsular War (1811).

General Wolfe The famous British soldier (1727–59) who defeated the French general, Montcalm, and took Quebec; he thus began the conquest of Canada.

Semele In classical mythology she was loved by Jupiter, the king of the gods. Juno, Jupiter's wife, was jealous of her, and by a trick persuaded Semele to get Jupiter to promise to come to her as he did to Juno. Jupiter was horrified by what he had promised, but he had to do as he had said, so he came with lightning and poor Semele was killed.

Arne Dr Arne (1710–78) was one of the most important of English composers. *Rule Britannia* comes from one of his works.

mollusc Shell-fish.

eau-de-Cologne A liquid perfume first made at Cologne, the city on the river Rhine, in Germany.

Chapter V. Maggie's second visit

Tom has hurt Philip so deeply that the quarrel between them cannot be made up. Maggie comes to visit Tom again and is attracted towards Philip, who thinks that she is 'a nice little thing'. On the first day of Maggie's stay, Tom takes her up to his room and makes her wait outside until he has dressed up as a fierce warrior. She laughs at this and does not notice Mr Poulter's sword, which Tom is wearing. He therefore draws the sword and, in demonstrating it, he brings it down on his foot, which he injures. He faints.

Maggie's sensitivity responds to Philip's, despite the obvious distance between the two boys. But the main focus is certainly on the drama of Tom's wound, and this again shows George Eliot's ability to write dramatic narrative.

There was no malignity . . . repulsion Philip was not
spiteful or evil-minded, but he could take a strong dislike to a person.
hectored Bullied; a word derived from the name of Hector (see note p.49).
wry-necked With a twisted neck – the head permanently on one side.
paternoster Lord's Prayer. 'Pater' means 'Father' and 'noster' means 'our'.
preconcerted arrangement i.e. he had arranged all the effects beforehand.
Bluebeard He was the man in the children's story who married several wives and murdered them. His last wife entered the room which he had forbidden her to enter, and so discovered his crimes and was saved from him.

Chapter VI. A love-scene

After Tom's wound is attended to, he begins to worry lest he should be permanently lame. He dare not ask about it because he is too frightened. Philip Wakem guesses that Tom will worry in this way, and he asks Mr Stelling, who tells him that Tom will soon be quite well again. Philip goes to see Tom and tells him this, and Tom is so grateful that the boys become friends for a while. One day, Maggie talks with Philip and promises to be like a sister to him; she caresses him as she does Tom. After she has gone home and Tom is well, the boys are less friendly.

This shows Philip's sensitivity on Tom's account, though we feel that he is already so drawn to Maggie that his actions spring from this. We are aware that any friendship between the boys can only be temporary, but we also sense that Maggie feels for Philip and that in view of the latter's withdrawn nature there is danger here.

sad privation Both boys were deprived of something; Philip of a normal life because of his deformity, and Tom, temporarily, of his power to walk.

Philoctetes One of the twelve Argonauts, led by Jason, who set out in their ship, the *Argo*, to find the Golden Fleece; he was a great friend of Hercules. He was wounded in the foot and the Greeks banished him because of the evil odour which came from the wound. Later, he was miraculously healed and killed many Trojans.

the grey colt . . . black sire Mr Tulliver warns Tom that although Philip is like his mother in ways and in appearance, he may still have some of his father's evil intentions.

Chapter VII. *The golden gates are passed*

Time passes; Tom is sixteen and is growing up in mind as well as in body. Maggie, too, although only thirteen, has been changed by her boarding school into a young lady. She sees Philip very seldom during these years. Mr Tulliver begins his lawsuit and Lawyer Wakem acts against him. One November day, just before Tom is due to leave Mr Stelling for good, Maggie comes to break bad news to him; his father has lost the lawsuit, and this means that he has lost all his possessions, including the mill. Worse than this, he has fallen from his horse and is desperately ill. The only person whom he recognizes is Maggie.

The climactic chapter in which everything changes. Childhood is over, and a kind of adulthood must be assumed, at least by Tom. Perhaps it is true to say that brother and sister have never been so close as they are here initially in adversity. It is poignant and dramatic, the mood one of sombre and distressing adjustment.

sweet illusory promises In childhood, it seems as if the world promises us many things; some of these promises are deceptive.
Eden The garden in which Adam and Eve, the first man and woman, were placed by God (Genesis, II).
meteor-like rapidity As speedily as a comet travels across the sky.
virgin razor His razor was as yet unused because he had no need to shave.
turnpike See note p.39.
accoutrements Things which belonged to his position.
prognostics Forecasts.

Revision questions on Book Second

1 What have you discovered about Mr Stelling and his wife from Book Second?
2 Show the cause and describe the progress of the dispute between Mr Tulliver and Mr Pivart. What were its results?
3 What did Tom Tulliver and Philip Wakem think of each other? How did they get on together?
4 What was Mr Poulter, and how does he come into the story?
5 Describe the second visit paid by Maggie to Mr and Mrs Stelling.

Book Third. The downfall

Chapter I. What had happened at home

When Mr Tulliver first knew that he had lost his lawsuit, he seemed to take the news very well. He imagined that a Mr Furley, who had a mortgage on the property, would buy the mill and the land and let him remain as a tenant so that, although he might have less money, he could still carry on. Unfortunately, Mr Tulliver had had to pay £250 when Mr Riley died, and he had also borrowed £500 when he had paid

Aunt Glegg her money; in addition Mr Tulliver had signed a document by which the man to whom he owed the money could have his furniture sold if he did not pay the debt. He wanted Maggie, and so he sent a letter to her boarding-school asking her to come home. Then he went to see his lawyer, Mr Gore. He was out but had left a letter for Mr Tulliver, who set out for home without reading it. Presently, he stopped his horse and began to read, thus learning that Mr Furley had sold the mortgage to Lawyer Wakem because he was in money difficulties himself; of course, he could not buy Mr Tulliver's lands. This news gives Mr Tulliver such a shock that he becomes ill and falls from his horse. Later, one of his men finds him unconscious. Maggie arrives home and her father recognizes her. The aunts, who came to see the stricken family, think that Tom should not be fetched from school, but Maggie decides to go for him. As they return, Maggie tells Tom about Lawyer Wakem, and Tom blames him for his father's condition and orders Maggie not to speak to Philip again.

This retrospective chapter fills in all the details of legal and economic failure which puts Mr Tulliver into the hands of Lawyer Wakem. Maggie shows her own strength of mind in going for Tom, and the latter shows his own obstinate and closed nature in forbidding Maggie to speak to Philip. Once again this is superb atmospheric writing – we now see a contrasting kind of family interaction.

expedients Means to an end; he could find many ways to prevent the world from knowing how bad he felt.

suretyship Being a security. Mr Tulliver had promised that if Mr Riley could not pay the debt of £250 (and when he had promised this there seemed no danger that Riley would not be able to pay), Mr Tulliver would pay the money for him.

eminently Extremely.

bill of sale If he could not pay his debts, his creditors would take the mill and its furniture.

sweeps the stage . . . sublime Tragedy represented on the stage usually deals with the affairs of kings and queens, but in spite of his comparatively humble position, Mr Tulliver's tragedy was equally serious.

tenacity of position Holding fast to one place.
straitened for money Finding it difficult to obtain money.
infantine satisfaction Childish pleasure.

Chapter II. Mrs Tulliver's Teraphim or household gods

Tom and Maggie arrive home to find a bailiff smoking in the
parlour. They go to look for Mrs Tulliver, who is taking out
all the china and linen and the silver teapot which she has
treasured for many years. She tells him that the aunts are
going to buy some of the things, and she blames her husband
for going to law and for spending her fortune. Maggie resents
this criticism of her father. When Tom sees Mr Tulliver, he is
very upset by his father's condition.

The pathos is deepened by the focus on Mrs Tulliver.
Family divisions immediately surface, with Mrs Tulliver
blaming her husband and Maggie, as we should expect,
passionately concerned to defend him and to show her love
for him.

Teraphim Household gods of the Hebrews, who consulted them
  as oracles who could fortell future events.
have the bailiff in the house The bailiff is the Sheriff's officer
  who stays in the house of a debtor until the debt is paid; his job
  is to prevent any of the goods from being removed.
bailies Bailiffs (d.).
chany China (d.).
egoistic resentment She felt strong personal anger at the
  attitude of her mother.

Chapter III. The family council

The aunts and uncles come to the mill to decide what can be
done to help Mrs Tulliver, who is very upset at having to part
with her treasured possessions. Mrs Deane says that she will
buy some of the best linen and china, but Mrs Glegg is angry
with Mrs Tulliver for bothering about such things. Mrs Glegg
wishes Tom and Maggie to hear what is said. Presently, when
Mrs Glegg speaks badly of Mr Tulliver, Tom tells the assem-

bled relatives that it would be better if they paid the money his father owed instead of blaming him, and so prevented his mother's possessions from being sold. Though Mrs Glegg admires Tom for the attitude he takes, she is irritated and again disparages Mr Tulliver, whereupon Maggie attacks them all bitterly. At that moment, Mrs Moss, Mr Tulliver's sister, comes, having heard of her brother's illness. She is very distressed and says that she and her husband would pay back the £300 her brother had lent her, if it did not mean that her husband must sell his farm to get the money. Mr Glegg thinks that Mr Moss should pay the money whatever happens, but Tom says that his father wished Mr and Mrs Moss to have the money and he must obey his wishes. In the end, this is agreed upon, and Maggie takes her relatives to find the note promising payment of the debt which Mr Moss had given to Mr Tulliver.

Even the chapter title is ominous with the present suffering and contrasts with that earlier unofficial family council when Mr Tulliver had pronounced on Tom's education and fallen out with Mrs Glegg. Tom's common-sense and practicality despite his education are well in evidence, and Maggie reacts spiritedly, as we should expect. But what emerges most clearly – apart from the family divisions – is the economic prudence of the relations, perhaps exemplified in Mrs Glegg's response to Tom's suggestion. The arrival of Aunt Gritty sparks further divisions, but it also shows Tom in an honourable light as well. Pathos, suffering, an atmosphere which reduces all and certainly brings further grief to Maggie, makes this one of the most moving and dramatically effective chapters in the book.

unbagged the bell rope tassels In those days each room had a rope made of velvet or such material, which was connected to a wire that rang a bell in the kitchen to summon a servant. When a room was not in use the ropes were rolled up into bags.

unpinned the curtains The curtains were fastened up to keep them from getting dirty.

livery-servant Servant wearing his master's uniform.

wolds Downs.

Ethiopians Inhabitants of Ethiopia, East Africa (once called Abyssinia).

cut jelly-glasses Glasses cut into facets that catch the light; these glasses were used by Mrs Tulliver to hold jelly.

compendious mode Form of expression for every emotion.

creasy form Her clothes had not been pressed and were full of creases.

pier-glass An ornamental mirror let into a wall.

Bath chair A wheeled chair for invalids, named from the city of Bath, in Somerset, England, a spa where they were much used.

from the parish The Tullivers might be treated as paupers to be looked after by public money.

flock-bed A bed stuffed with fibrous material of cotton and wool.

family predominance Mrs Glegg was the oldest sister, who had always told Mrs Tulliver what to do.

'ull Will (d.).

trusten Trust (old form of word).

Golden Lion A public house in St Ogg's.

E.D. Mrs Tulliver's initials before she married, when she was Elizabeth Dodson.

codicil An appendix attached to a will.

cupped This was the term used when blood was drawn from a patient.

assignees People to whom property is assigned or handed.

alienating Transferring property from one person to another.

lawing Going to law.

Chapter IV. A vanishing gleam

As they look into the chest, the iron rod which is keeping up the lid falls with a crash. The shock brings back Mr Tulliver to consciousness, and for a while he recognizes his family and can remember most of the things that have happened. Presently, he lapses into unconsciousness again.

This is a considered stress on the isolation of Mr Tulliver in the world of the unconscious and now in the world of the conscious where he has lost everything.

spasmodic rigidity At times, Mr Tulliver would give a sudden convulsive movement and then become rigid again.

deeds Documents which show ownership of lands.

make a shift Make an attempt.
sanative Health-giving.
lesion Injury.

Chapter V. Tom applies his knife to the oyster

Tom decides to consult Mr Deane, his prosperous uncle, about getting work. Mr Deane talks a great deal about how he rose to a good position in the world without the kind of education which Tom has had and which Mr Deane despises. He is not very helpful. As Tom returns home, he sees a bill advertising the sale of the contents of Dorlcote Mill. When he reaches home, cross at the way he has been treated, he is annoyed by Maggie's attempt at a joke and scolds her indignantly for her behaviour to her aunts. Maggie is heart-broken.

Tom shows his sense of responsibility and also his insensitivity to his sister's needs. Maggie's dependence on him is as strong as ever.

irrepressible indignation Tom could not help feeling indignant at the way his father had behaved.
the mind . . . self-flattery A boy like Tom, who was a practical child, not dreaming what might happen.
auditing Making an official examination of documents.
Themes Short essays.
Euclid See note p.44.
Blair's *Rhetoric* A celebrated book used in the eighteenth century to teach composition and argument in speech. The author, Hugh Blair, was a famous Scottish preacher.
New Tariff A new list of goods on which duty must be paid if they are brought into the country.
hair-powder In the eighteenth century men and women powdered their hair with white powder.
usher in a school i.e. assistant master.
charity boy A boy who paid no fees at school and did servants' work in return.
round Rung.
broadcloth Fine woollen cloth with a smooth surface.
flinty shingles Hard pebbles.
Dominie Sampson An eccentric schoolmaster in the novel *Guy Mannering* by Sir Walter Scott.

Lucy Bertram Another character from *Guy Mannering*.
premature despair . . . present Older people know that time
  will heal grief and despair, but they are unable to persuade the
  young that this is so.

Revision questions on Book Third, Chapters I–V

1 Trace the steps by which Mr Tulliver becomes fully
aware of the extent of the calamity which has befallen him.
2 What are the reactions of (a) Mrs Tulliver, (b) Tom, and
(c) Maggie, to the troubles which come upon them?
3 What is your opinion of the behaviour of Mrs Tulliver's
sisters during her trouble?
4 Why is it important that Tom should find the paper
given by Mr Moss to Mr Tulliver? Describe the incident
when they are searching for it.
5 Describe the interview between Tom and his uncle, Mr
Deane.

*Chapter VI. Tending to refute the popular prejudice against the
present of a pocket-knife*

On the day of the sale, Tom and Maggie sit with their mother
in their father's room, dreading lest he should become conscious and hear the noise made by the auctioneer and the
crowd. Fortunately, he remains unaware of all that is happening. When it is over, Kezia, the maid, comes to tell Tom that a
man is asking to see him; it is Bob Jakin, to whom he once
gave a pocket-knife and who, to show his continued friendship, has come to offer him nine sovereigns, all that remains of
the £10 which was given to him as a reward for putting out a
fire in the mill where he worked. He has fitted himself out with
goods that he can carry in a pack and intends to travel
through the countryside selling them. Tom and Maggie are
very touched by the offer of the money, but refuse it.

  Another moving chapter, finely atmospheric in terms of the
suffering for Tom and Maggie as the sale goes on. Bob Jakin's
offer shows his common humanity, a touchstone for George

Eliot's own moral appraisal of character throughout *The Mill on the Floss* and her works in general.

'scrazing' Scratching, rubbing.
suffer a waste of tissue through evaporation Perspire, sweat.
tablets Small flat pieces of ivory or slate upon which people wrote in the old days, using a sharply-pointed tool.
gen Gave (d.).
arter After.
squerrils Squirrels. This is Bob's pronunciation.
istid Instead.
jaw Talk (d.).
cause of their parting quarrel The cause was that Bob cheated at a game and refused to give Tom the halfpenny which he had won, and Tom had fought him.
yead Head (d.). See note p.27.
ax Ask (d.).
shy at Hurl a stone at.
raff Abbreviation of 'riff-raff', rabble.
pursuant Following.
tenting Tending.
doused Put out the fire.
genelman Gentleman. This, again, is Bob's pronunciation.
suvreigns Sovereigns. English gold coins, each worth £1 and each having on one side the head of the English king or queen who reigned when it was minted.
kettle of broth Saucepan of soup.
pigs' chitterlings Small entrails of the pig, which can be eaten.
packman A pedlar who travels the countryside with his pack of goods for sale.
paradisaic Resembling paradise or Heaven.
wescoat Waistcoat (d.).
round-sterned Dutchmen Merchant ships from Holland; the Dutch built their vessels with the stern or back part almost round.
'quinetance' acquaintance.
'feel nohow' Embarrassed.
Do Deceiver. Bob means that he sometimes cheats.
let him in a bit Cheat.
transported Sent out of the country as a punishment. Convicts were transported to Australia in the early days.

fleabites i.e. small injuries.
hev Have (d.).
flux Flow.

Chapter VII. How a hen takes to stratagem

Mr Tulliver begins to get better and it is hoped that he will recover. His mill and lands are now to be sold, and Uncle Deane, who has begun to take an interest in the affairs of the Tullivers, thinks that the firm which employs him, Guest and Co, may buy the mill and allow Mr Tulliver to stay on as manager. The only danger is that Lawyer Wakem may bid against Uncle Deane at the auction. Mrs Tulliver decides, therefore, that she will go secretly to see Lawyer Wakem and beg him not to bid. At this time, Wakem has no intention of trying to get possession of Dorlcote Mill, but when he learns from Mrs Tulliver that Guest and Co are interested, he decides that it might be valuable to him. He tells her that he might buy it and employ her husband, but she declares that her husband would never work for him. Wakem's mind is now made up; he will buy the mill, if it is possible, and, in addition to getting something worthwhile, he will get revenge on Mr Tulliver for all the abuse he has had from him.

The ingredients in this chapter are a mixture of comedy and pathos. Mrs Tulliver unwittingly plays into Wakem's hands and ensures that the quality of her husband's suffering continues, thus exacerbating the position.

paralytic obstruction i.e. a clot of blood which made Mr Tulliver unable to move.
allocaturs Certificates of approval signed by a judge.
filing of bills in Chancery i.e. placing the bills on record in the court presided over by the Lord Chancellor.
legal chainshot Ammunition for the lawyers.
elastic commodity Uncle Glegg had bought a waistcoat which would stretch; he is getting fat.
bankrupt A man or woman becomes bankrupt when the law declares that he or she is unable to pay debts; his or her goods are sold and the money shared among the creditors. For every pound the bankrupt owes them, they may get only a certain percentage,

more or less, according to the amount. The matter is managed by the court on behalf of those to whom the money is owed.

unequivocal disproportion There could be no doubt about the difference between how much Mr Tulliver had and how much he owed.

portentous anomaly Unusual event which foretold disaster.

spencer Short coat, worn by women.

ketchup This sauce is made from mushrooms, tomatoes and other ingredients.

receipts Recipes (for making the pickle).

eidolon Phantom.

hypothesis . . . diabolical agency Mr Tulliver thought that he could never be wrong, so that when misfortune came to him, he at once believed that it must be the devil's work, since he was convinced that nothing could happen to him accidentally.

unexpected mince-meat He is completely destroyed.

fly-wheel A heavy wheel in a machine, regulating its motion.

a priori See note p.45.

t'abuse This is very tactless of Mrs Tulliver.

pike Greedy freshwater fish.

roach Freshwater fish.

personal animosity Resentment against a man for a reason which affects only the man who feels resentful.

cattle-feeder Man who fattens cattle.

Old ladies' wills People would hint that lawyers made their fortunes by persuading old ladies to leave them money when they made their wills.

sang froid Cool indifference and self-possession (Fr.).

cockpit Place where cock-fights were held (see note on 'strongest spurs', p.46).

versed Experienced.

that pitiable . . . net Mr Tulliver, like the bull, was strong in one way, but pathetically weak when trapped in all the difficult points of law.

Yellow candidate Man who tries to become a Member of the English House of Commons. Yellow and Blue are taken as the names of the rival parties.

vituperative rhetoric Speeches attacking the other candidate.

highly-blent Well-mixed (see note on 'blent', p.30).

filed Smoothed.

maxims Proverbs, wise sayings.

mural monuments Pieces of stone or wood fixed to the wall of a
church in memory of the person whose name and record are
carved upon it.

chiaroscuro parentage Parentage whose characters contrast
with each other; chiaroscuro is the term used in painting or
drawing to mean the treatment of light and shade.

fly-fishers . . . subjectivity of fishes Men fishing with flies
sometimes catch no fish because they fail to take into account
the feelings and taste of the fish.

Chapter VIII. Daylight on the wreck

One January day, Mr Tulliver feels well enough to go down-
stairs again. His family dread what will happen when he
discovers that his mill and lands have been bought by Lawyer
Wakem. Luke, the farm labourer, accidentally lets him know
that he has been made bankrupt and he soon realizes that his
possessions have been sold. At last Mrs Tulliver tells him that
Wakem has bought the mill and is willing to employ him as manager. Tom resents his father's becoming the lawyer's servant.

This position becomes acute now that Mr Tulliver is more
mobile again. But there is more pathos than anything else in
this sequence, and we feel that although one disaster has been
negotiated the next one is not far away, given the nature of Mr
Tulliver's temperament.

moithering Worrying (d.).

'mushed' Silly (d.).

Saturnalian Unrestrained, exciting. The Saturnalia was an
ancient Roman festival in honour of the god, Saturn, in which
even the slaves took part.

bankrupt See note p.60.

susceptibility Feeling or capability.

Nemean lion Fierce lion which, according to Greek legend,
troubled the town of Nemea, in Greece; it was killed by the
hero, Hercules, as the first of his labours.

quarto Bible This is a large bible, roughly 20 cm by 25 cm
(8 in. by 10 in.).

fly-leaf Blank page inserted usually at the beginning of a book.

in abeyance In suspension. Mr Tulliver's pride was not seen
during this time.

Chapter IX. An item added to the family register

Mr Tulliver wanders about the places he has known since he was a boy and talks to Luke about them. One evening he waits impatiently for Tom to come home from work, and, when he comes, he tells him that he has decided to accept Wakem's offer of a job. Then he orders his son to fetch the family Bible and to write a statement that he will have revenge on Lawyer Wakem, if ever he gets the chance.

The revenge motif, so terrible to Maggie, is here spelled out by the obdurate Mr Tulliver. The terrible thing is that it places a burden upon Tom.

banyans Trees found in India and Ceylon; they produce roots from the ends of branches, which grow down into the soil instead of into the air.

Zambesi Great river of Africa flowing into the Mozambique channel of the Indian Ocean.

rust on the wheat Red mould which destroys the wheat; it is caused by a fungus.

malting Preparing the barley for brewing.

treadmill A large wheel driven by people treading on the steps made in the rim; it was formerly used as a form of punishment in prisons.

Revision questions on Book Third, Chapters VI–IX

1 How does Bob Jakin reappear in the story? Recount the information he gives Tom.
2 Describe Mrs Tulliver's visit to Lawyer Wakem. What was its result?
3 How does Mr Tulliver learn that he has been made bankrupt? What is the effect on him?
4 What fresh entry was made in the Tullivers' family Bible and why?

Book Fourth. The Valley of Humiliation

Chapter I. A variation of Protestantism unknown to Bossuet

The author talks about the ruined villages which are to be found on the banks of the River Rhone. She does not like them because they are mean and dreary, and not like the ruined castles on the banks of the River Rhine. She thinks that her readers may feel like this and find the story of the Tullivers and Dodsons mean. She wants them to feel the narrowness of their lives so that they may realize the effect on Tom and Maggie.

This is a very deliberate authorial interjection into the narrative. It is somewhat pedantically done – it holds up the story – but the analogy certainly points up the constrained nature of the provincial life which George Eliot is bent on exposing.

The Valley of Humiliation The valley through which Christian went in Bunyan's *Pilgrim's Progress*.

Bossuet A famous French preacher (1627–1704).

Rhone A river which rises in Switzerland, finally flowing into the North Sea.

grunter Pig.

pious recluse The religious hermit.

timid Israelite Jews were persecuted in the Middle Ages. George Eliot is probably thinking of the novel *Ivanhoe*, by Sir Walter Scott, in which a timid Jew and a hermit appear.

gig of unfashionable build Old-fashioned gig (see note p.24).

without side-dishes Without any of the pleasures.

A vigorous superstition . . . Tullivers The kind of religious or moral belief which makes those who hold it punish themselves does not seem likely to have a connection with such ant-like people as the Dodsons and the Tullivers.

emmet Ant.

ascertainment Making certain.

deductively Arguing from a general idea, i.e. that they were British Protestants, to a particular idea.

heresy Theory against what is acknowledged by the authorities to be the truth.

unimpeachable will Will which could not be questioned.

Obedience to parents . . . utensils Note that the rules for the cleaning of a house are as important as those for the conduct of life.

fromenty Food made of whole wheat boiled in milk.

fellowship A special position in the constitution of the college of a university.

total absence of hooks Some seeds have hooks in order to fasten them into the soil; the seeds of Mr Tulliver's religion had no hooks and so did not remain with him.

Chapter II. The torn nest is pierced by the thorns

Mr Tulliver settles down to life as Wakem's manager. Tom does not like his work, and finds his mother's regrets for the past and his father's continual depression very trying. Mr Tulliver keeps always in his mind the idea of saving to pay back the money he owes. He sees that Maggie is growing up and he wonders how she is to meet any man who will make her a good husband. He does not wish her to marry a very poor man, as her aunt, his sister, had done.

The sufferings continue in their various degrees. We always warm to Tulliver's humanity – here his concern for Maggie's future – and his sense of integrity, the idea of paying back the money ultimately. And we are aware too of Tom's gradual small accumulations, since he too shares his father's sense of honour, or at least is aware of his father's priority.

transient strength Strength which comes temporarily to a sick man.

emotive intensity His strongly-felt emotion had now given way to dull despair.

usual precocity Maggie had always been very knowledgeable for her age.

massy Heavy.

kindle up Come to life.

incubus Nightmare or heavy weight of oppression. In the Middle Ages it was the name of a demon who appeared to sleepers.

pillory A wooden frame with an upright post. This had holes, through which the head and hands of a person to be punished were placed and secured.

egoism The habit of thinking of oneself as the most important thing in existence.

hollow resonance The room echoed the footsteps of those who walked over it because it was so bare.

Chapter III. A voice from the past

Bob Jakin, now established as a packman, brings Maggie some books to replace those sold when her father went bankrupt. Among them is *The Imitation of Christ*, by Thomas à Kempis. Maggie is greatly impressed by this, and decides to follow the old writer's advice and forget her own selfish wishes and devote herself to helping others. She persuades a shopkeeper to give her sewing to do so that she may make money to help pay her father's debts.

The return of Bob Jakin is instrumental in giving Maggie something to live for. But she is fighting her own nature and we sense that the battle will be a hard one. Moreover, this decision drives her back upon herself, making her even more deprived socially. Despite her discovery, the note struck is a sombre one.

jasmine a plant with white waxen flowers that have a sweet perfume.

paroxysm of rage Outburst of temper.

irretrievably disgraceful Maggie was afraid that when her father was almost mad with anger he would commit some dreadful act which could not be undone.

brindled Tawny in colour, with streaks of another colour.

sawney Fool or simpleton (d.).

'Keepsake' The name of a magazine for women published in the early and middle years of the nineteenth century.

George the Fourth King of England 1820–30. He was known as 'The First Gentleman of Europe', but he has also been described as 'an undutiful son, a bad husband and a callous father'.

depressed cranium Flattened skull.

sot Sat (d.).

say-so Small sum of money (d.).

Punch show Punch and Judy, the puppet show for children, telling of the trials of Punch and his dog, which is always played by a real dog.

tolerating . . . in general i.e. making no fuss because there were so many things around him that he thought unnecessary.

gingerbread No thief could tempt Mumps with a tit-bit.

go wi' the ferrets Bob does not go hunting rabbits with ferrets (see note on 'ferrets', p.27).

Burke's grand dirge Edmund Burke (1729–97) was a great political thinker and writer. He lamented the fact that the courtesy and nobleness expected of a knight in the Middle Ages no longer existed.

Télémaque A narrative written by Fénélon (1651–1715), a famous French writer. It tells of the adventures of Telemachus.

Scott's novels Sir Walter Scott (1771–1826) was a native of Scotland and a great writer; most of his novels are historical, like *Ivanhoe, Kenilworth* and *The Talisman* (see note on 'Dominie Sampson', p.57).

Byron's poems Lord Byron (1788–1824) was a poet who was as famous on the continent of Europe as in England.

temporary provision . . . Catholicism The Protestants who died for their religion in the reign of Mary prevented the restoration of the Catholic faith in England.

Smithfield Queen Mary Tudor disapproved of the Reformation in England brought about by her father, Henry VIII, and she tried to bring England under the power of the Pope again. She persecuted the Protestants and burnt many people, including Thomas Cranmer, Archbishop of Canterbury. Most of them died at Smithfield, in London.

Eutropius A Latin historian who died about AD 370. He wrote a history of Rome in a simple style, probably intended for schools.

Virgil See note p.49.

syllogism A form of argument.

The Spectator Periodical containing essays, produced in the eighteenth century by Joseph Addison and Richard Steele.

Rasselas A novel by the famous writer Dr Samuel Johnson (1709–83), who also compiled a great English dictionary.

Gregory's Letters These were written by Pope Gregory I (540–604), who sent St Augustine to convert Britain to Christianity.

Thomas à Kempis The monk (1379–1471) who wrote the famous religious book, *On the Following or Imitation of Christ*.

evil perturbations Worries which come from thinking too much about oneself.

mysticism A form of religion claiming that one can gain union with God by solitary thought; this doctrine was first put forward by a Spanish priest, and was condemned by Pope Innocent XI in 1687.

quietism A form of passive religious mysticism.

tonsured head Head of a monk with the centre shaved.

crinoline vortices A vortex is the hollow circular form which is taken by water or other liquid when it is rotated; everything near is then drawn into it, so this means that the gentlemen must not be attracted by women. Crinolines were the long dresses with enormous stiffened skirts that ladies wore in those days.

Faraday Michael Faraday (1791–1867) was a chemist and philosopher who lectured and wrote on many subjects, especially the condensation of gases.

ekstasis Standing out (Greek). These people find alcohol takes them away in imagination from the sordid world in which they live.

Tree of Knowledge The tree which, according to the Bible story, grew in the Garden of Eden. God forbade Adam to eat of its fruit, lest he should learn to know good from evil (Genesis, III).

Revision questions on Book Fourth

1 Describe the life at Dorlcote Mill after it had been sold to Lawyer Wakem.

2 How did Bob Jakin prove himself to be a true friend?

3 Give the title of the book from which Maggie found the greatest comfort. What did she learn from it?

4 Show how narrow-minded the Dodsons were.

Book Fifth. Wheat and tares

Chapter I. In the Red Deeps

When Maggie is seventeen she sees Philip Wakem again. He comes with his father to the mill, but they do not actually meet. Later, Maggie goes for a walk and finds Philip waiting in the Red Deeps. He has made a portrait of her when he saw her at Mr Stelling's house, and Maggie is touched and flattered by this. She does not realize that he is in love with her, but she feels that it would be wrong to meet him secretly as he wishes. However, she consents to think it over and to meet him once more to give him her answer.

The pathos of Maggie's lot is exemplified in this chapter. Philip represents sensitivity and culture, both of which her soul cries out for. But this release is of course conditional upon her conscience, and we can see the pitfalls ahead in view of the male Tulliver attitude towards the Wakems. And of course we remember, and it bulks large in Maggie's consciousness, the oath taken on the family Bible.

face towards the wall Maggie was determined not to think of herself; she would not even look at herself in a mirror, but turned it face to the wall.

garment of Silence The author is personifying silence as a person in a cloak edged with tiny bells.

wild hyacinths More often known as bluebells.

for a penance This is a reference to the punishment which a man inflicts upon himself to show how sorry he is for having done wrong.

The Pirate Name of a novel by Sir Walter Scott (see note p.67).

Chapter II. Aunt Glegg learns the breadth of Bob's thumb

Tom is doing well in business and his Uncle Deane is pleased. Uncle Glegg, too, decides that he may help him later on, although he afterwards decides that it will be better not to interfere with his nephew's progress. Bob Jakin suggests that Tom should join him in sending some goods abroad in order to sell them and make money. Tom asks his father for money to do this, but Mr Tulliver is so worried by the thought that the money may be lost that Tom decides not to touch their joint savings but to ask Uncle Glegg to lend him £20. Bob goes with him and not only persuades Uncle and Aunt Glegg to lend the money, but also sells some of his goods to Aunt Glegg. After a while, Tom has made nearly £150.

There is some delightful humour in this chapter, with Aunt Glegg and Bob Jakin vying with one another in terms of commercial opportunism. In fact economics are the key here, since Tom's own responsibility plus the expansion through Bob Jakin indicates the coming settlement so dear to Mr Tulliver's heart.

Hecuba The wife of Priam, King of Troy, and mother of ten sons, including Hector (see note p.49).

excursus Excursion, digression. Mr Deane talked about things not really connected with the subject.

bottoms Ships.

spooney Weak-minded.

carguy Cargo.

briny Brainy, clever; this is Bob's pronunciation.

unembarrassed loquacity Bob talked a great deal without feeling that people might not want to listen to him.

Aaron Brother of Moses, who led the Israelites out of captivity in Egypt. Moses was not a good speaker, and as this would be a disadvantage in a leader he had his brother to speak for him (Exodus, VII. 1).

taters Potatoes (d.).

ates Eats (d.).

stand surety See note on 'suretyship', p.53.

adapted to the moral . . . them Mrs Glegg was quite near Bob, but she spoke in a loud voice to show how superior she was to him.

solicited by a double curiosity . . . wait Two things made her inquisitive, but as Bob would not satisfy her curiosity about the one, she had to try to find out the other.

Princess Victoree Princess Victoria, later Queen of England.

put it me out Put it out for me.

shupercargo This is Bob's pronunciation of 'supercargo', a name given to a man, usually an officer, in a merchant ship; his job is to look after the cargo and all the commercial business of a ship during a voyage.

bathos A figure of speech in which a serious remark is followed by an ordinary one, which makes the whole thing ridiculous; also known as anti-climax.

Chapter III. The Wavering balance

When Maggie meets Philip again at the Red Deeps she tells him that she cannot see him any more. He tries to persuade her that she should allow him to give her books and help her to have more knowledge of music and literature. At last he pleads that she should not banish him from the Red Deeps and mentions the possibility of a chance meeting.

Our sympathy is with Maggie, and with Philip, but we realize that this idyll cannot continue. The scene is beautifully described and written with a warm identification. We are acutely aware of the needs of each, and that these needs differ in degree.

seductive guidance of illimitable wants At first Maggie gave up everything that did not fit in with her new life, but when she abandoned this idea she found there was no limit to the things she wanted.

opal A semi-precious stone which is sometimes milky in colour and sometimes shot with various colours.

Hamadryad In Greek legend this was a wood nymph.

sotto voce Spoken under the breath or in an undertone (Ital.).

dull quiescence Placid calmness. Maggie seemed to show no spirit of rebellion, but to accept her fate.

Chapter IV. Another love-scene

Maggie continues to meet Philip, and one day in the following spring, when she is complaining that in novels it is always the 'blonde' heroine who wins the hero's love from the dark-haired girl, he suggests that she may win the love of some handsome young man away from her fair-haired cousin, Lucy Deane. Maggie is hurt at this, and Philip is led to tell her of his love for her and to win from her a confession that she loves him.

The inevitable occurs. Philip's confession of love for Maggie and his dependence on her draw forth a like response, and we are aware just how dependent she is too – Philip provides that cultural basis which she so lacks at home. The tension is generated by the fact that we feel, as Maggie certainly does, that these are snatched precious moments.

Corinne Heroine of a French novel of that title by Madame de Staël (1684–1759).

tenth muse In Greek mythology the nine muses were the

goddesses who presided over poetry, music, dancing and the other arts.

baize Coarse woollen material.

Rebecca A dark-haired Jewess who is a character in the novel *Ivanhoe*, by Sir Walter Scott; her story is a sad one.

Flora MacIvor She is also dark-haired; the heroine of Sir Walter Scott's *Waverley*.

Minna Heroine of a comedy by the German dramatist Lessing (1729–81).

besotted Intoxicated, made foolish.

cloven tree Tree which has been split in two.

Chapter V. *The cloven tree*

Maggie has a constant fear that her father or Tom will see her with Philip. This she knows is most unlikely to happen, but Tom guesses that she has been seeing Philip when she becomes very confused at a statement by Aunt Pullet that she has frequently seen Philip coming from the Red Deeps. The next afternoon Tom comes home unexpectedly from the office just as Maggie is leaving to meet Philip. He forces her to tell him everything that has happened, and, by threatening to tell their father, makes her promise to have no further communication with Philip. When she says that she must see him once more, Tom goes with her to the Red Deeps. There is a violent scene between the two men, and later Maggie accuses her brother of being hard and un-Christianlike. She is secretly a little relieved at parting with Philip.

This is the climactic scene, with Tom reacting as we would expect and Maggie deeply injured and humiliated by his words and actions. For Philip we feel pain at his being made to suffer in this way. What has been apparent throughout, that Tom has doubts about Maggie and that she as a woman is the weaker vessel who can do little or nothing to help the family, is here emphasized. The revenge promised has not been forgotten.

incalculable states of mind Feelings which no one can guess beforehand.

channel of fatality Means by which Tom was to learn about Maggie's actions.

crowflower A plant with rather dull bluish flowers, usually known as crowbill.

bell, Belle; young and beautiful girl.

superstitious repugnance Most primitive races dislike anything out of the ordinary because they believe that it will bring bad luck.

Pharisee Member of a religious sect of the Jews in Christ's time. They kept all the forms and ceremonies of Jewish law, but were not always careful to do what was good and kind. They attacked Christ on many occasions.

Chapter VI. The hard-won triumph

At last the time comes when Tom is able to tell his father that he has made enough money by trading to add to what they have saved and pay off his debts. A meeting of the creditors is called; Mr Tulliver is speechless with joy, but he recovers and rejoices most of all that he can now be free of Wakem. Maggie admires Tom, in spite of the coldness with which he treats her.

One of the few scenes of untrammelled happiness in the novel. Maggie is again in the subordinate position, though if feeling for her father alone counted she would not be.

guttural enunciation Deep, throaty way of pronouncing words.

juvenile history The story of Bob's childhood.

irrelevant exclamation Remark that had no connection with what he was talking about.

Chapter VII. A day of reckoning

Mr Tulliver attends the dinner for his creditors, and is proud of Tom, who speaks to them. Afterwards he rides home, hoping to see Wakem and show him that he is free from debt again. Wakem is just leaving the mill when he arrives there; Mr Tulliver loses his temper, and when Wakem is thrown from his horse, he seizes the opportunity to thrash him. Maggie stops her father. Mr Tulliver goes to bed immediately, and next morning he dies. Tom and Maggie are friends once more in their common grief.

This superb chapter moves from joy to tragedy, with dramatic, graphic description. Maggie plays a positive part, but we feel that it is too late. The irony of the chapter heading is felt on the two levels of experience – the paying off of the creditors and the passionate and wrong-headed paying back of Wakem. Maggie's intervention represents her enlightened humanity. But as usual she is frustrated. The coming together after division of Tom and Maggie is a deliberate prefiguring of the end of the novel.

Hotspur See note p.22.

perhaps be forsaken . . . impudence Mr Tulliver thought that perhaps Lawyer Wakem would be less confident in his actions.

hysteric Hysterical, violently emotional.

Revision questions on Book Fifth

1 How did Maggie meet Philip Wakem again when they were grown up, and how did the meeting affect her?

2 Describe Bob Jakin's visit to Aunt Glegg and show the consequences of the visit.

3 What kind of things did Bob Jakin sell? How do you know this?

4 How did Tom discover about Maggie's meetings with Philip, and what did he do?

5 What have you learned of Tom's character from these chapters?

Book Sixth. The great temptation

Chapter I. A duet in paradise

It is two years later; Mrs Tulliver is keeping house for Mr Deane and Lucy, her sister, Mrs Deane, having died some time before. Lucy, now eighteen, is with her lover, Stephen Guest, the son of the head of the firm where her father was once an employee but is now a director. She tells him that Maggie is leaving the situation in a school, which she had held for two years, and is coming to stay with her mother and the Deanes for a while. Stephen Guest, who has never seen Maggie, describes what he thinks she is like. He is quite wrong, but Lucy, for a joke, pretends that he has given an accurate description.

With the passage of time the reader is moved on to a different level of society which forms a contrast with what has gone before. There is a lightness in tone which matches the (at present) uncomplicated lives of Lucy and Stephen. Since Maggie is the centre of our interest, narrative expectation is raised by her imminent return.

'King Charles' Toy spaniel dog with silky coat and long ears, named after King Charles II, who kept them as pets.

Minny The dog.

Hercules See note on 'Nemean lion', p.62.

da capo From the beginning (Ital.).

band Belt (around Lucy's waist).

ratafias A kind of biscuit, flavoured with brandy in which the kernels of cherries, peaches or almonds have been soaked.

buckram See note p.28.

round-robin A petition with the names of those signing arranged in a circle so that no one may know who signed first and so be accounted the leader.

Beatrice The woman who was loved by the Italian poet Dante (1256–1321), who wrote about her in his long poem, *The Divine Comedy*.

brandy-cherries Cherries cooked in brandy.

proxies These stand in place of persons who cannot be present at a ceremony.

Lucifer A name for Satan, who rebelled against God and was banished from Heaven to Hell. Milton told the story in his famous poem, *Paradise Lost*.

Turpin Dick Turpin, the famous highwayman of the early eighteenth century, who rode his mare, Black Bess, along the road to York and robbed any travellers he could find.

falsetto Artificial tone of voice, higher than the voice normally used by the singer.

The Creation An oratorio telling in words and music the story of the creation of the world; it was written by Haydn, a famous Austrian musician (1732–1809).

Adam See note on 'man's rib', p.39.

fugue A musical work in which the theme is repeated by the different instruments.

rotten boroughs MPs who represented these boroughs in the English House of Commons bought the right to do so.

Raphael See note p.21.

chiffonier Small sideboard (Fr.).

her small egoisms . . . it Even when she thought of herself she was considering how she helped other people.

Judas-kisses i.e. kisses that are deceitful and insincere. Judas kissed Christ in order that the men to whom he had betrayed his Master might know Him (Luke, XII. 47).

Chapter II. First impressions

Maggie arrives and meets Stephen Guest. After her two years as governess she finds very trying the light conversation required in society. Stephen Guest is very much impressed by her, especially as she is not in the least like what he had been led to expect. He takes her for a row on the river with Lucy, and when they return they find that Uncle and Aunt Pullet have come to visit Mrs Tulliver. Aunt Pullet wants Maggie to have an evening dress.

The nature of Maggie's continuing deprivation is evident, but what is so successfully conveyed here almost from the beginning is the sexual attraction between herself and Stephen, though this is of course not acknowledged at this stage by either. By a wonderful transition, she has grown up to be very attractive though, as we might expect, not in a conventional way.

merino Soft woollen fabric.

Marie Antoinette Queen of Louis XVI, King of France, at the time when the French Revolution began. Marie Antoinette was guillotined by the people's government.

Cinderella Heroine of the fairy tale by the French writer, Perrault. She was badly treated by her step-sisters, but her fairy godmother intervened and in the end she married the prince.

Pinnock A writer who lived in the nineteenth century and produced an educational catechism, i.e. questions and answers on various subjects.

gleemen Singers who sang glees, i.e. songs for three or more voices.

second-sight A power which some people, especially those of the Highlands of Scotland, are supposed to possess of seeing events which are happening in other places far away from them.

set . . . by the ears He has angered them by using the forms and ceremonies of the High Church.

Southey Poet and biographer (1774–1843), at one time the Poet Laureate of England.

Cowper An English poet (1731–1800); among his poems are *The Ballad of John Gilpin* and *The Task*.

Bridgwater Treatises Eight discussions on religion written by various clergymen in accordance with the will of the Earl of Bridgwater, who died in 1829.

downy-lipped alumnus A newcomer to a college of a university who has not yet needed to shave as he is so young.

à propos Concerning (Fr.).

Purcell One of the greatest English composers, who wrote a great deal of church music (1658–95).

Nut-Brown Maid One of the English ballads sung in the Middle Ages.

Chapter III. Confidential moments

After Stephen Guest has gone, Maggie is excited and unable to prepare for sleep. Lucy comes to her room and they discuss Guest. Then Lucy mentions that Philip Wakem is coming to the house the next day; because of her promise to Tom, Maggie is unwilling to meet him and is forced to tell Lucy the story of her love affair with Philip. The author hints that, because she knows of this, Lucy will be unable to realize that love is growing between Maggie and Stephen Guest.

Maggie is disturbed by feelings which she cannot properly understand. But with the mention of Philip the tension rises for her and for the reader. Maggie is still conditioned by the promise of the past, but her confiding in Lucy is a master stroke by George Eliot. Lucy is thus able to make up her own romance about Maggie, while Maggie, unknown to herself and to Lucy, is beginning to fall in love with Stephen.

toilette table Dressing-table.

absolve me Free me. A priest gives absolution to a sinner who has confessed his sins and repented.

Sir Andrew Ague-cheek A foolish knight in Shakespeare's play *Twelfth Night*; he drinks every night with Sir Toby Belch, and when Sir Toby says that he is adored by Maria, the maid, Sir Andrew says, 'I was adored once' (*Twelfth Night*, II. iii).

Chapter IV. *Brother and sister*

Maggie goes to see Tom, who is lodging with Bob Jakin and his wife, a very small woman. Bob's mother also lives with them. Maggie asks Tom to free her from her promise not to see Philip without his consent. They almost quarrel again, but at last are reconciled, so that Tom says she may meet Philip at Lucy's house. She suspects that Tom is in love with Lucy.

Humiliation again for Maggie, but at least she gets a guarded response from Tom. There is a lack of generosity of spirit about Tom which we have always sensed.

physiognomy The science of finding about a person's character from a study of his face (see note on 'physiognomist', p.47).

Dutch doll See note p.46.

overshoot him Make him exaggerate and say too much.

tilted bottle A bottle which is tilted cannot keep the liquid which has been put in it.

glumpish Sad.

tow'rt Near, towards it (d.).

alienation Coolness between people, unfriendliness, estrangement.

sacrament of conciliation In childhood they used to share a cake as a kind of pledge that they were friends again.

bell-rope See note p.55.

Chapter V. *Showing that Tom had opened the oyster*

Tom has an interview with Mr Deane. The firm is very pleased with him, and he is to be given a share in the business. Tom also has a proposal to make. He had promised his dying father to try to get possession of Dorlcote Mill, and he suggests that Mr Deane might buy it and put him, Tom, in charge. Mr Deane does not think that Lawyer Wakem will be willing to sell.

Tom's progress is charted and his ambitions are spelled out. We are aware of the fact that the man's world is being set against the woman's – that Tom can work (perhaps this helps to make him even narrower) but that Maggie has no outlet for her feelings.

oyster A quotation from Shakespeare's *Merry Wives of Windsor* (II. ii). It is spoken by Pistol, the soldier, to Falstaff.

deliberate impartiality He took snuff carefully, giving a pinch to each nostril in turn, as if he had determined to be fair to each.

wheel of fortune The goddess of Fortune had a wheel as her symbol to show how a man's circumstances may change from good to bad or bad to good.

two ears of corn . . . before A quotation from *Gulliver's Travels*, Book II, Chapter IV. The words were spoken to Gulliver by the King of Brobdingnag, who ruled the nation of giants.

flashy fellows Men who try to appear smart and clever, but are unreliable.

premium Reward.

Pelley's bank Tom had learned that Pelley's bank was in difficulties and had warned Mr Guest and his uncle, and so saved their firm from losing a great deal of money.

Revision questions on Book Sixth, Chapters I–V

1 Give Stephen Guest's imaginary description of Maggie. In what ways is it inaccurate?

2 What is Aunt Pullet's attitude to Maggie as shown in these chapters?

3 Describe Maggie's visit to Tom when she wishes to be allowed to see Philip Wakem again. What is your opinion of Tom's attitude?

4 Explain Mr Deane's proposal to Tom and state Tom's answer.

Chapter VI. Illustrating the laws of attraction

Maggie is introduced by Lucy to the society of St Ogg's and is much admired. Philip does not appear for a while, as he had gone off on a sketching expedition before he knew of Maggie's arrival. Stephen Guest is very much attracted by Maggie, although he pays careful attention to Lucy. One evening, when he knows that Lucy is out, he comes to bring her some music so as to be alone with Maggie. It is now obvious that Stephen and Maggie are falling in love.

Philip's entrance being delayed gives more time for Stephen to pay Maggie more attention – and in her natural feminine way she appreciates this though without fully understanding her own feelings.

eye-glass The single glass for one eye, worn in those days by smart young men.

billiard-room The game of billiards was just coming into fashion, and the idea of a special room in which it could be played was new and smart.

glass of fashion Example which all the other fashionable ladies followed. The phrase is used by Ophelia in Shakespeare's play *Hamlet*, III. i.

took some exception to They did not approve of Maggie's complete honesty in answering questions.

gaucherie Awkwardness (Fr.).

intervals An interval is the distance between two given musical notes.

Novalis The pen-name of a German writer of romances, von Hardenberg (1772–1801), who thought that life ought to be poetry made real in conduct.

Hamlet, Prince of Denmark The hero of Shakespeare's play. His father's ghost appeared to him to demand revenge for his murder by his own brother, Hamlet's uncle. Hamlet had been in love with Ophelia, daughter of the king's old counsellor, Polonius (see note p.48).

Miss Sophia Western She is the heroine of the novel *Tom Jones*, by Henry Fielding, one of the greatest novelists of the eighteenth century.

tempo time, in music (Ital.).

reticules Handbags made of cloth used by the ladies of the day.

direct taxation i.e. income tax.
improvisation Composing music as one plays.
minion Darling (Fr., 'mignon').
monomania Madness on one subject only.
cribbage A card game.

Chapter VII. Philip re-enters

Maggie meets Philip again when he comes to call on Lucy. As they talk, Maggie remembers what he once said about her taking away a lover from Lucy; she then realizes her position with Stephen. Presently Stephen arrives and there is music. Philip sings a song to let Maggie know that he still loves her, but soon he begins to be jealous of Stephen and to suspect his feeling for Maggie. The young people are interrupted by Mrs Tulliver, who comes to tell them that lunch is ready. Mr Deane asks Philip whether his father is interested in farming, and later Lucy gets Mr Deane's permission to ask Philip to find out.

When she does meet Philip things become somewhat clearer in her own mind. Philip's sensitivity plus his own frustrated feelings for Maggie are productive of tension. Lucy's unwitting actions are calculated to stir up trouble of which she is completely ignorant.

illimitable Unending, a long visit.
nullified . . . felt Maggie did not feel that she was doing wrong in welcoming Philip, since she believed that he would help her to overcome her feeling for Stephen.
in the morrow of it He felt that the scene in the Red Deeps had occurred only on the day before.
make myself a world . . . do. Maggie wished that she could keep separate her personal feelings and her work, as a man must do.
Masaniello. An opera by Auber. Masaniello, the hero, was a Neapolitan fisherman who, in 1647, led a revolt against the Spanish rulers of Naples.
minor The key in music in which the scale has a minor third, giving a plaintive tone.
Beggar's Opera Amusing musical play by John Gay

(1685–1732). Its hero is a highwayman, and most of its characters are thieves and vagabonds, or the gaolers who look after them.

canterbury A stand, with divisions for holding music.
antidote A substance given to counteract the effect of poison.
Shall I . . . Fair? A quotation from a poem by George Wither (1588–1667), used as the title of a song.
The Tempest Music for Shakespeare's play of that name.
decanter An ornamental glass bottle for holding wine or spirits.
sugar-plums Balls of boiled sugar.
accompt book Account book.

Chapter VIII. Wakem in a new light

Lucy speaks to Philip about the mill, and he decides to ask his father about it. He invites him to his painting-room and tells him of his love for Maggie. Wakem is very angry and leaves him. Later, Wakem talks to Philip again and consents to his marrying Maggie if she will have him. He also agrees to sell Dorlcote Mill. Mr Deane is puzzled but pleased by what Lucy has accomplished.

In the event Wakem, faced with the possibility of his son's marrying, proves more flexible than we might have supposed, though we do recall Maggie's going to his assistance when he was attacked by Mr Tulliver.

sanctum Study; Philip's own private room.
double eye-glass Spectacles.
ridiculous rancour Stupid quarrelling.

Chapter IX. Charity in full dress

The great day of the bazaar comes. Maggie has only a simple dress to wear, but its very simplicity makes her beauty more obvious and distinguishes her among the elaborately-dressed ladies of St Ogg's. The gentlemen come to buy at her stall and the ladies believe that she is trying to attract their attention. Mr Wakem buys some goods from Maggie. Then Philip sees Stephen come to speak to Maggie, and when, later, he pretends to have been snubbed by her, Philip calls him a hypocrite. Dr Kenn, the vicar, sees Maggie and senses that she is in some kind of mental distress. Lucy tells Maggie that Mr Deane will be able to buy back Dorlcote Mill and tries to persuade her to continue to stay with her; she is amazed to learn that Maggie has already taken another post as a teacher. She is also very hurt and upset when Maggie says that she cannot marry Philip because of Tom's strong antipathy to him.

Another pivotal chapter, with Maggie on display, Philip's suspicions confirmed in his own mind, and Lucy out of her depth. The exchanges are full of tension, based on deception and concealment. Maggie's fear is now a fear of herself as much as anything.

Bazaar A function planned to make money for a good cause; ladies make and sell goods for the highest price they can get.

heraldic animals Strange creatures represented in the coats of arms of the great lords.

seigniors Lords, possessors.

oriel See note p.38.

celestial breasts of charitable ladies The hearts of ladies who are working for the good of others should be worthy of heaven.

hypothetic claims In theory, any lady of St Ogg's might claim Stephen Guest as a possible husband.

cajole Flatter, persuade.

fez A close-fitting felt hat with no brim but with a tassel, worn by Turks and Egyptians.

coxcomb Vain, presumptuous person.

thinking of the frosty Caucasus A quotation from Shakespeare's play, *Richard II* (I. iii. 295); it is spoken by Bolingbroke, Richard's cousin, to his father, John of Gaunt, when Bolingbroke has been banished for six years.

giant Python A great snake, supposed by the Greeks to have sprung from the mud which covered the earth after the deluge.

canonicals All their splendour of dress.

cheval-glass Full length, swing looking-glass.

Correggio's cherubs Reference to baby cupids painted by the Italian artist of the sixteenth century, who took the name of Correggio because he lived there.

Chapter X. The spell seems broken

Maggie goes to the dance at Stephen's home. By this time
Stephen is jealous of Philip. At the dance he comes to Maggie
and takes her to walk in the conservatory. He is overcome by
his feeling for her and kisses her arm; she declares that he has
insulted her. This moment makes her feel that she is free from
any temptation to take Stephen away from Lucy. Next morning, Philip comes to see her, and she tells him that her consideration for her brother is the only thing that prevents their
marriage.

Stephen's overt sexual approach is too much for Maggie
who, though unconventional in some ways, is a girl of her time
when it comes to strict morality. But it helps her to fight off
what has become an increasing temptation.

laid aside her black Lucy, like Maggie, had been in mourning
for Mr Tulliver.
caps and cards The older ladies wore lace caps and played
cards.
pretentious etiquette Formal code of manners. The country
dance allowed no one to take notice of rank and class.
conservatory Glass building filled with plants and attached to a
house.
Parthenon A temple in Athens sacred to the goddess Athene,
rebuilt by the great ruler Pericles; it is still in existence.

Revision questions on Book Sixth, Chapters VI–X

1 How does George Eliot show the growth of the feeling
between Maggie and Stephen Guest?
2 Describe Maggie's meeting with Philip Wakem at the
house of Mr Deane.
3 How is Tom's desire to return to Dorlcote Mill helped by
Lucy's plans? Explain fully.
4 Give an account of the Bazaar at St Ogg's. What are the
various opinions expressed about Maggie?
5 Describe the dance at Park House. Why was it important
to Maggie?

Chapter XI. In the lane

Maggie goes to stay with her father's sister, Mrs Moss. There Stephen Guest comes to see her and tries to persuade her to throw aside all her obligations and responsibilities. She admits that she loves him, but says that, in spite of this, they must part, and they say goodbye.

Maggie's flight to Aunt Gritty shows how strong that temptation is. Stephen's appearance shows that he has crossed the social barrier, that he will do anything to be with Maggie, and his journey here prepares us for the elopement. We have always felt Maggie's strong sympathetic affinity for her aunt and the measure of it is seen here.

avatar Appearance of a god in earthly form.
tacit engagements Engagements which have not been formally acknowledged, but are understood.

Chapter XII. A family party

Maggie is to visit Aunt Pullet. Lucy brings her news that Jetsome, Mr Wakem's employee in charge of Dorlcote Mill has been thrown by his horse when drunk, and so Mr Wakem wants Tom to go back to the mill at once. There is a family tea-party at Aunt Pullet's, and everyone tries to persuade Maggie to give up the idea of taking another post. Tom joins the party and is very friendly to Maggie. On the way home, Lucy tells Tom of the events which have made it possible for Mr Deane's firm to buy the mill. She thinks that this will make him change his attitude to Philip, but he merely answers coldly that Maggie must please herself; he will have nothing to do with Philip Wakem.

Lucy's scheme works out, but Tom's attitude, despite the changed situation, is hardened as regards Philip. Maggie's determination to take a post away from the area indicates the nature of her inner fears.

last limb of an eclipse i.e. the last bit of shadow across the sun.
cockatrices Fabulous serpents; supposed to be able to kill by a glance.

dangerous way The stairs were highly polished.
flax A blue-flowered plant from which linen is made.
Indy i.e. India.
muffineer A dish to hold muffins.
lawing See note p. 56.
holland Unbleached linen, brownish in colour (see note on 'holland sheets', p. 20).
conscious recitude of purpose Firm feeling of doing the right thing.
staff and a baton i.e. staff to support a man and a baton to conduct others, as a conductor conducts an orchestra.
metamorphose Change into another form.

Chapter XIII. Borne along by the tide

Lucy wants Maggie to have some boating on the Floss. Stephen and Philip are to take it in turns to go with them. One day she arranges that Philip shall take them, and then decides to go to a nearby town so that Maggie and Philip will be alone. Philip is ill, however, because he is tortured by his suspicions about Maggie's feeling for Stephen, and he asks Stephen to take his place with the ladies. Stephen takes Maggie in the boat, and because of her worry is able to take her so far down the river that they cannot get back that day. He pleads with Maggie to elope with him. At last they are picked up by a Dutch vessel going to Mudport and have to spend the night on board.

This is yet another pivotal chapter, with the might-have-been element strongly present. If Philip had not been ill . . . if Lucy had not believed that Philip and Maggie would be alone . . . The chapter is full of tension, with Maggie's role largely passive as she is 'borne along by the tide'.

sufficient ostensible motive The headaches would give him an excuse.
Laceham Courier The local newspaper.
Scotland Here it would be possible for them to be married, since Scottish law does not require the same residence in the country as English law.

poop Stern of a ship.
nectar The wine of the gods in Greek mythology.

Chapter XIV. Waking

Maggie has troubled dreams, and when she wakes she is
horrified at the thought of the pain that she will bring to Lucy
and Philip. When they land, Stephen plans that they will
travel north and be married, but Maggie refuses and says that
she is returning home. Stephen does his best to persuade her
to marry him, but she is determined not to do so and sets out
for home.

Note the significance of Maggie's dream and the fact that
she is still the virgin of St Ogg's. That dream conditions her
waking, and her strong morality, always evident, takes over. A
compassionate irony surrounds her. Maggie's independent
spirit, the sense of betrayal that she feels over Lucy, is movingly
intense.

native honour i.e. honour which was part of his nature.

Revision questions on Book Sixth, Chapters XI–XIV

1 Describe Maggie's visit to her father's sister, Mrs Moss.
What do you learn from this chapter of the Moss
family?
2 What subjects were discussed at the family party at Aunt
Pullet's house? Give an account of the conversation.
3 How did Philip's conviction that there was some feeling
between Maggie and Stephen contribute to the final
catastrophe of their supposed elopement?
4 Describe what happened to Maggie from the time she set
out with Stephen to go to Luckreth until she arrived home
again. What did the various people who knew her think had
happened?
5 What is your opinion of the conduct of Stephen Guest in
this incident?

Book Seventh. The final rescue

Chapter I. The return to the mill

Maggie returns to the mill where Tom is now master. Bob Jakin had seen her land with Stephen at Mudport, and Tom fears disgrace for the family. When he sees her, he shows that he is near hating her and turns her from the house. Mrs Tulliver hears this and she goes with Maggie; they decide to go to Bob Jakin's house. Bob brings her his baby daughter, which he has called Maggie after her, and tries to do all he can to please her.

Again we are aware of the common humanity of Bob, the inflexibility of Tom, and the somewhat surprising reaction of Mrs Tulliver which proves that Maggie is not just her father's daughter.

wish to pry Desire to find out someone else's business.
He'll none go away He will not go away.
make no jaw Will not talk (d.).

Chapter II. St Ogg's passes judgement

If Maggie had returned to St Ogg's a little later, as Stephen's wife, no one would have condemned her, but since she had returned unmarried, the gossips had much to say about her treatment of Lucy and her setting a trap to catch poor Mr Guest as a husband. Meanwhile, Maggie is tortured by anxiety about Stephen, as well as about Lucy and Tom. She begins to do plain sewing again in order to pay Bob for her lodgings. Lucy is ill with shock. One day, Maggie goes to see Dr Kenn, the vicar, and tells him her story. He has read a letter from Stephen to his family, in which he tells his father about trying to persuade Maggie to elope with him. Dr Kenn promises to help Maggie to face a suspicious world, but he secretly hopes that she may at last marry Stephen.

This chapter probes the difference between appearance and reality – what the local community thinks and what has actually happened. By these standards Maggie is really innocent, but gossip will never have things that way.

post-marital trousseau They thought that Maggie would buy clothes for her new life after her marriage.
feminine gender i.e. the women in the community.
satinette Thin kind of satin.
put up for the borough i.e. become a candidate for election to Parliament.
casuists People who judge each case on its merits, regardless of principles.

Chapter III. Showing that old acquaintances are capable of surprising us

Aunt Glegg, unexpectedly, refuses to believe evil of Maggie, and after Stephen's letter has been received, she prepares to attack anyone who speaks badly of her. Mrs Tulliver tells Maggie that Lucy is a little better, but Maggie is still worried about Philip. At last she receives a letter from him in which he expresses his faith in her and his continued love for her; he begs her that she will not reproach herself about him.

The support of Aunt Glegg and Philip in their different ways is an affirmation of George Eliot's faith in human nature.

legatee Person to whom a legacy is left by will.
fair play was a jewel An old saying which means that everyone has a right to justice.
hereditary rectitude Aunt Glegg had inherited a keen sense of what was the right thing to do.
'having' See note p.26.

Chapter IV. Maggie and Lucy

Dr Kenn tries to find a situation for Maggie, but he discovers that both men and women of St Ogg's are spreading slander about her and consequently no one will employ her. He therefore offers her a post as nursery governess to his children and she gratefully accepts. However, he has just lost his wife, and at once there is more discussion, and the ladies are afraid that

he will marry Maggie. Maggie is still very worried about Lucy
and longs to see her; then, one hot night, Lucy comes secretly
to Bob's house, and the cousins meet and are reconciled.

This faith is exemplified in the practical Christianity of Dr
Kenn, but defeated of course by the evil of gossip. Lucy, too,
despite all her suffering, is living evidence of essential good-
ness.

imputations Accusations which they made against Maggie.
piquancy in evil-speaking Some of Dr Kenn's parishioners
found evil and gossip made life more entertaining, as a piquant
sauce makes food more appetizing.
self-exaltation in condemning When some people condemn the
misdeeds of others, they enjoy feeling how good they themselves
are.
superfluous incense The ladies of his congregation had paid Dr
Kenn great reverence when he had no need of it.
crotchets Strange whims and fancies.
an apostle A reference to St Peter's denial of our Lord
(Matthew, XXVI. 69–76).
alleviation Lessening.
added its momentum i.e. increased their sympathy.

Chapter V. The last conflict

At last Dr Kenn is warned by one of his parishioners about the
gossip concerning Maggie and himself, and he reluctantly tells
her that he will try to find a situation for her outside St Ogg's.
She is very upset by this, and she is upset, too, by a letter from
Stephen Guest imploring her to marry him and reproaching
her for the misery she is causing him. One rainy night, as she
sits in her room in Bob Jakin's house, tempted to the limit of
her endurance and almost wishing that her life would end, she
suddenly realizes that water is seeping under the door. She
warns Bob and his wife, and then sets off in a boat for Dorlcote
Mill. The current is strong, but it seems as if she is divinely
guided, for she reaches the mill and finds Tom marooned in
an upper room. He takes the oars from her and rows towards
St Ogg's, but there is wreckage in the river and this is driven

against the boat, and it is sunk. Brother and sister are drowned, and when they are found, they are clasped in each other's arms.

The catastrophe contains some of George Eliot's finest and most graphic writing. Her sense of the flood is evocative and imaginative, but the tragic element – of needless loss – is ironically conceived. There is an element of contrivance in the fact that brother and sister are brought together by chance, but chance has played a major part in the novel anyway.

equinox Periods in March and September when day and night are of equal length.
leaded panes Small panes of glass fastened in window frames made of lead.

Conclusion

Five years later all the damage caused by the floods has been repaired. Tom and Maggie are buried with their father in the churchyard, and their tomb is visited by the two men who loved Maggie: Stephen, who after a long while has at last married Lucy, and Philip, who lives with his memories for the rest of his days.

The final irony of their lives is seen in this aftermath, which contains the register of earthly change but the permanence of death.

'In their death they were not divided' The reference is to David's lament for Saul and Jonathan (2 Samuel 1:23).

Revision Questions on Book Seventh

1 Describe Maggie's return to Dorlcote Mill after she has come back from York and had an interview with Tom.
2 What was St Ogg's judgement on Maggie after her adventure with Stephen Guest?
3 Trace the thoughts in Maggie's mind (a) just before Lucy's visit to her, and (b) just before she realizes that the river is in flood.

4 What attempts to help Maggie were made by Dr Kenn? Why did they fail?
5 What is your opinion of the final scenes of the book? Do you consider that they are too melodramatic?

The characters

Maggie

So ended the sorrows of this day, and the next morning Maggie was
trotting with her own fishing-rod in one hand and a handle of the
basket in the other, stepping always, by a peculiar gift, in the
muddiest places, and looking darkly radiant from under her beaver-
bonnet because Tom was good to her. (I, v)

The quotation above demonstrates at once Maggie's obsession
with her brother and underlines George Eliot's early wish to
call the novel 'Sister Maggie'. Maggie is the centre of *The Mill
on the Floss*, and all our reactions radiate from her. George
Eliot was never to forget the experiences of her own childhood
and her closeness to her brother Isaac, from whom she was
estranged following her liaison with George Henry Lewes.
She was to write of that later with a wistful nostalgia which
survived the break:

But were another childhood world my share,
I would be born a little sister there.

There is thus a close identification with Maggie throughout,
and below I outline what seem to me to be the main traits of
her character; the enquiring and sensitive student will find
more than I indicate, for we live with Maggie through the
entirety of the novel's action, sharing her tribulations, identifying with her anguish, delighting in her increased self-
awareness and her rare moments of happiness and fulfilment.
The way in which George Eliot traces Maggie's transforma-
tion from ugly duckling to attractive woman is a triumph of
artistic skill and of truth to human nature, but initially we are
concerned with the child who lives in a family-dominated
world where her *cleverness* and *quickness* are subdued by
criticism and convention.

Maggie, like her creator, was not made to stand alone. She

is largely *dependent* on Tom and his reactions to her needs, and the early chapters of the novel examine the nature of that dependence. She longs for his return from school, but, because of her *dreamy* and *self-absorbed* nature, neglects to see that his rabbits are fed; they die, and she suffers his anger when he finds out and castigates her. This first incident sets the pattern for so many of their future exchanges, with Tom hard and Maggie blameworthy. Maggie is *impetuous* and *capable of temper*, as she shows by the indiscriminate shearing of her hair, and (there is some *jealousy* here) when she pushes Lucy into the mud after Tom has paid his cousin rather more attention than Maggie thinks necessary. Her *passionate* nature is seen in many incidents, and her Fetish – the doll with its nail-scarred head – is sufficient testimony to the wayward and headlong indulgence of her moods. This passionate side to Maggie embarrasses Tom but delights her father, whose arms are always open to receive his 'little wench', all too often, alas, as she turns to him with feelings bruised by lack of understanding on the part of others. Although her *cleverness* goes largely unappreciated by Mr Riley, Mr Stelling takes to her, and her visits to that gentleman and his two pupils, Philip and Tom, provide evidence of the sharpness of her intellect. Here, too, her *sensitivity* is apparent, allied to the *warmth of her nature* towards Philip for his generosity in reassuring Tom that his foot has not been permanently injured by the sword. Maggie is easily hurt, has a capacity for emotional suffering herself, and when she feels herself rejected by Tom escapes to the illusory world of gipsy life where she foresees herself as a queen. This incident demonstrates another facet of her character, her *unworldliness and innocence*. The social boundaries of St Ogg's are narrow, Maggie's dreams and visions are large, but they are not rooted in reality. Maggie, then, is *sympathetic* and *affectionate* though, in childhood, *jealous* where Tom is concerned. Her affectionate nature is well in evidence in her responses both to Philip and to Bob Jakin. Her warmth stands her in good stead when the family crisis occurs; Maggie is despatched to bring Tom home and to break the news to him of his father's stroke. Throughout this terrible period her *loyalty* to her father is never in question, and indeed her sense of *duty* remains a strong motivating force throughout her life, as we see much later when she determines to renounce Stephen. She is *deeply emotional*, and Philip provides an outlet for her feelings and her *aesthetic* and *artistic* sense (they share a love of art, literature and music); to Philip Maggie shows something akin to *maternal affection*, even when Tom humiliates Philip (and his sister) after their meetings in the Red Deeps.

Maggie has an inherent *sense of right* which is not overturned by the Dodson pride, as it is in Tom; she passionately rejects the swearing of revenge on Wakem and his family, her *humanitarian* sensibilities grossly offended by the mindless severity of the ritual and its implications. It is Maggie who acts to save Wakem from something worse than flogging at the hands of her stricken father, Maggie who forces Stephen to turn back and who leaves him in the hotel at Mudport, and Maggie who acts in the final sequence, helping Bob to loose the boat so that she can row off in an attempt to rescue Tom. All these actions contradict the impression of her that Tom has – that she is feckless, will-less, lacking in a sense of responsibility. Maggie, in effect, takes responsibility where others would fail to do so; she does what she has to do, compelled initially by her warmth of feeling and an outgoing nature which needs love in return for her own commitment. Her later conditioning owes much to her reading of Thomas à Kempis, for from this she learns *renunciation* of self – an underlining of her inherent sense of duty – and thus unconsciously prepares herself for the momentous decision to give up Stephen because of the injury she is conscious of having done to others. What Tom sees as weakness in Maggie is really *impressionability*. Her longing to be loved is seen in her appreciation of Stephen's moving a footstool or adjusting her music for her; in having politeness, refinement, culture at her elbow, so to speak, where before she has been accustomed to a reduced way of life, little or no conversation, a sense of unrelieved despondency. It takes *moral strength* and *courage* to do what Maggie does, not because she has to face the small world after doing it, but because she gives up the man she *does* love. We must not forget that Maggie is only nineteen when she meets Stephen, that she is *inexperienced* in the ways of the world, that she is *susceptible* but not yet sexually awakened. The result is a conflict of emotion and reaction as, for instance, when Stephen kisses her arm in the conservatory, and she suddenly withdraws it and accuses him of insulting her. And this is the man she loves! But the reaction is not extraordinary if we consider it carefully, for the *guilt feelings* are here plain to see, and they are to remain with Maggie throughout her association with Stephen. Her *conscience* is ever-present to her, her sense of *wrong-doing* paramount as, for example, when she walks in the lane with Stephen at her Aunt Gritty's. Her *sexual awareness* is held in check by her knowledge of her own *frailty*; she drifts with Stephen, yields to temptation but fights through it to the anguish of *decision*. So distraught is she by the strength of will needed to carry through that decision that she gets into the wrong coach at Mudport. Maggie's sympathetic imagination makes her acutely cognizant of the sufferings of others, but by a sublime stroke of irony George Eliot makes her the real Virgin of St Ogg's as distinct from the Virgin of the legend. Spiritual, idealistic, misunderstood, condemned for her courage, deserving of love, shelter and understanding, Maggie finds herself befriended anew by the loyal Bob Jakin and, ironically, her mother and Aunt Glegg stand by her, too. She cherishes Lucy's understanding and forgiveness, feels for Philip in his own lonely anguish, and resists, despite the intensity of her longings, the desire to join Stephen when she receives his letter.

Maggie's bright, mercurial, volatile temperament is conditioned to sorrow, blame, and a kind of injustice, the kind that condemns what appears to be weakness from the standpoints of pride and insensitivity. The confines of her lot are seen against the fullness of her emotions and the richness of her mind. She falls, and yet she does not fall, from grace; her sins are transitory and are never of the spirit. There is no one in her immediate family circle, not even her father, who has any conception of her feelings or of the damming up of her nature by the pressures of convention, restriction and prejudice. I have deliberately chosen not to quote in this section on Maggie, since the student who really gets to know the novel well will find his or her own particular quotations to support the character points made above and others which are only hinted at here. We follow Maggie's inner turmoil through to the end, from those first wanderings up and down by the river which cause her mother so much worry, to the final inundation; we are with her in her spiritual awakening, at the onset of love, in social disgrace, in ultimate reconciliation. In a sense we are thankful, so strong is our identification, that she does not live; yet we feel the waste, the tragedy, the deep, deep dissatisfaction at her fate. A forgotten writer of the time, Ashford Owen, said in the preface to her moving and sensitive novel *A Lost Love* (1855) that 'an almost illimitable hope' lies behind what is called 'the despair of youth'. Maggie lives through despair, and her abiding hope, that she will be re-united with Tom, is illimitable in its human and spiritual strength.

Tom Tulliver

Still he was very fond of his sister, and meant always to take care of her, make her his housekeeper, and punish her when she did wrong. (I, v)

Tom Tulliver, the be-all and end-all in Maggie's young life, shares some qualities with her. He has a strong sense of family loyalty, though it is rather different from Maggie's, and he has a firm idea of duty, again different in quality and kind from that of his sister. He finishes at the Academy and is sent to Mr Stelling's on the advice of his father's friend Riley. Confronted by the puzzles of Latin and Euclid, Tom, who is by nature an outdoor boy, finds little to sustain him except the contemplation of a return home and trips with Yap, his dog, and, of course, the companionship of Maggie. His capacity for anger is early shown when he learns that Maggie has forgotten to ensure that his rabbits were fed. He is a boy who knows that he will inherit a man's world, and consequently he never treats Maggie as an equal; he is not merely older, he is, by virtue of his maleness, superior. A certain pattern emerges in his treatment of Maggie throughout their childhood; she can be humiliated whenever Tom feels that he is in the right or whenever she has offended him. An early example occurs when Lucy comes to visit them and Tom shuts Maggie out from their play, thus inadvertently causing Lucy to be pushed into the mud by Maggie and precipitating the latter's flight to the gipsies.

Tom has something of his father's quickness in temper and change of mood, and he can hurt Maggie merely by not calling her 'Magsie', the name he uses to indicate approval. But his basic attitudes towards life, authority, responsibility, status, do not change; they merely harden in the face of adversity. He is obstinate, like his father, and wrong-headed like him too, but the latter quality, which takes the form of moral severity rather than uncontrolled temper, passes unnoticed in the outside world, which only sees an upright youth intent on putting the family fortunes to rights. Tom has the family pride, and asserts it; he has strength of will, and imposes it, more particularly upon Maggie. There is no more unpleasantly moving sequence in the whole novel than that in which Tom upbraids Maggie and Philip for their secret meetings. It is not that he takes a sadistic pleasure in hurting either of them; rather is it an arrogant assertion of what Tom considers to be right action. It is a shocking display of insensitivity, the more shocking because it comes from a young man who ought to have been educated by his own suffering to a just and humane appreciation of the feelings of others. We see the measure of Tom when he swears to be revenged at his father's instigation – 'write as you'll remember what Wakem's done to your father, and you'll make him and his feel it, if ever the day comes. And sign your name Thomas Tulliver' (III, ix). Thus Tom consents to what is morally wrong, yet later judges Maggie by a superficial code of what is morally right. We remember that Tom had disliked Philip, and this again shows one of the less pleasant aspects of his personality – his lack of compassion, humility, human sympathy.

Tom is proud, arrogant, willing to take responsibility, as he demonstrates when he goes to see Mr Deane and accepts a subordinate position as a start; by his own efforts he works himself up into a position of trust and authority and proves himself an opportunist, availing himself of the chance to do some trading on his own account thanks to Bob Jakin. These are commendable traits, and it must be conceded that Tom, though oppressed by his father's incapacity, is never bowed down by it. He assumes the mantle of adulthood, takes over the role of head of the family with unremitting application; it makes him dour and it emphasizes his narrowness. He had no patience with the frailty of others, being blind to his own obduracy but seeing Maggie's weakness in what she says and does. Consequently when Maggie commits a 'sin' which can be measured his reaction is one of righteous indignation, and he shuts her out from his protection and his life.

Yet there is a certain nobility of response in Tom – to him, family is all, hence his determined and resolute inflexibility over Maggie's 'disgrace'. We must not forget that maturity is thrust upon him in youth, unexpectedly, and with tragic immediacy, and that he is capable of generous action. He cancels his Aunt Gritty's debt to his father despite the hostility of the aunts and uncles, and he seeks to provide for his mother and Maggie. But we cannot forget that other, dominant side; even as a boy Tom is without humour, selfish, and intolerant of others, though seeming to be good-natured at the Stellings'. He has to rule, as we see from his attitude towards Maggie, Philip and Bob Jakin, although he bribes Mr Poulter for the loan of the sword, Tom does not know the meaning of the word 'temptation'. Thus he often seems to the reader to be dehumanized, since some of the human failings and feelings experienced by us are unknown to him. He is essentially practical, though the emergence of that practicality is delayed by the meaningless academic disciplines which leave him unfulfilled until he has to earn his own living. He has the noble aim of getting the Mill back into the family, and achieves it. If we are not sympathetic towards Tom for the most part, it is because we cannot see fully into his feelings if, indeed, his feelings go that deep. Maggie remains the core of our involvement, and we see Tom largely through her eyes and reactions.

Mr Tulliver

'Come, come, my wench,' said her father soothingly, putting his arm around her, 'never mind; you was i' the right to cut it off if it plagued you; give over crying; father'll take your part.' (I, vii)

Whereas Tom has his father's obstinacy and Maggie has her father's warmth and impetuosity, the presence of Maggie's undoubted intelligence is not explained by a like presence of the equivalent in either Mr Tulliver or his wife. Mr Tulliver chose Bessie Dodson, as he tells Mr Riley, because she was none too bright, but an appraisal of Mr Tulliver's actions tells us that he is none too bright either. He is slow-thinking, argumentative, set on Tom having an 'eddication' but in no way clear as to what that 'eddication' needs to encompass. The Mill has been in his family for generations and he has a deep pride in its possession, but he hasn't the sense either to keep out of litigation or to accept rulings once they are imposed. Thus he is involved with Dix and Pivart, and part of his ambition for Tom is to equip him to deal with lawyers like Wakem who, he believes, serve 'Old Harry'. It is ironic that Tom's instruction at Mr Stelling's should be so divorced from the sharp cut and thrust of the law which Mr Tulliver so hates yet wants for his own. Mr Tulliver's slowness is revealed in his discussion with Riley, but we also note his affection for Maggie and his appreciation of her loyalty to Tom. His pride in himself makes him resent the patronage of the Dodson aunts, particularly Mrs Glegg, from whom he has borrowed money. His impetuosity moves him to repay the money, which he can ill-afford, and he drives over to Basset to get Moss to repay him in turn; of course Moss can't afford to do so and

Tulliver, his affection for Gritty deeply felt despite her descent in the world, forbears from pressing the claim. To his great credit he maintains this attitude, impressing it upon Tom after his partial recovery from his first stroke.

His warmth to his 'little wench' is always evident, but he can be stern and adamant in the home. Unlike his son, he has a sense of humour, but he is so beset by his worries as to be irascible and irrational, as we see in his flogging of Wakem. He is proud and quick-tempered, a curious balance of warm feelings which can overturn into loss of control. When he is on the way to recovery after his first seizure and comes to realize what has occurred – that he is now in his arch-enemy's hands – he resolves to abase himself and to do his best for the sake of Bessie and the children, but the deep fires of anger and humiliation at his lot cannot be put out, and they smoulder into the unworthy wish of revenge through the agency of his son.

Tulliver's pride in Tom when he pays the creditors is great, for his own pride in himself and his independence is restored; we see early in the novel the way that pride manifests itself in his mental rehearsals of what he will say to impress his hearers. But throughout his nature is against him; when Pivart and Wakem defeat him at law, his self-containment is as remarkable to himself as it is to others who know him. We sense, however, that the explosion cannot be long delayed, and we wonder at the corrosive effects of such self-repression. They are evident when Tulliver rides over to St Ogg's and, with an almost premonitory urge, writes to ask Maggie to come home the next day; it was as well that he did so, for Gore's letter which informs him that Wakem holds the mortgage on the Mill ruins his world and his physical death begins. Yet we find it hard to be too critical of Tulliver, for although he is wrong-headed, blind to effects, proud, obstinate, responsible for his own downfall, he is at the same time a generous-hearted man, warm, kind, moved where others would be indifferent or hard. In his prime he is reduced to imbecility, apathy and finally inarticulate rage and death. He never passes beyond our sympathy.

Mrs Tulliver

She was thankful to have been a Dodson, and to have one child who took after her own family at least in his features and complexion, in liking salt and in eating beans, which a Tulliver never did. (I, vi)

Mrs Tulliver is the youngest of the Dodson sisters, and lives her adult life very much aware of the superior positions held by those sisters, Mrs Glegg, Mrs Pullet and Mrs Deane. She is slow-thinking, limited and conventional in attitudes, aware all the time of having married beneath herself, at least by the standards of her sisters. She has a genuine pride in Tom, for his physical appearance makes him a Dodson, but Maggie is her despair, and her fears that Maggie will one day fall into the water carry an unconscious prophetic insight. Verbally she is no match for her husband, and she cannot cope with the caustic directness of Mrs Glegg or the tearful hypochondria of Mrs Pullet. She has a mother's possessiveness over Tom, fearing that he will not be well-fed and cared for at the Stellings', but is reassured after her visit; a mother's embarrassment, too, where Maggie is concerned, feeling horror and shame before her sisters when Maggie appears with her shorn locks. Mrs Tulliver in reaction to the first crisis is a pathetic figure, bowed down when the bill of sale is put into effect, humbled before her sisters as they sit in judgement on her husband's failure, bemoaning the loss of her material possessions and the loss of status attendant upon such disgrace. She appears weak, self-indulgent in her grief, so much so that Tulliver, when he gets back his reason, feels compelled to humble himself in his turn and accept his position under Wakem. But before that Mrs Tulliver – she is aptly compared to a hen – undertakes the foolish journey to Wakem which ensures that he *will* buy the Mill, a thought but scarcely present in his mind before that. Even this incident underlines a character trait: Mrs Tulliver is not contriving or designing – she is in fact innocent, simple-minded in her approach. And in a curious way this prepares us for the one even more positive action in her life – her standing by Maggie despite Tom's condemnation of his sister. Mrs Tulliver is not negative; she has a mother's instinct, and defends her young. She is a pathetic, amiable, limited woman, yet her own brand of obstinacy and loyalty shows that she has more character than we would be inclined to allow her – and perhaps more than her family realize.

Mrs Glegg

Mrs Glegg emitted a long sort of guttural sound with closed lips, that smiled in mingled pity and scorn. (I, vii)

Mrs Glegg is the most colourful and articulate of the Dodson aunts, with a bitter and ironic turn of speech. A fine-looking woman of about fifty (though thought by Tom and Maggie to exemplify the type of ugliness) she speaks her mind with acid directness, is inquisitive, independent, and easily persuades herself that she has been insulted. Her exterior hides not merely the inbuilt Dodson pride, but also a kinder heart than she would be prepared to own to. We may deplore Aunt Glegg's attack, brusquely and uncompromisingly delivered, on Mr Tulliver's plans for Tom's education, but we have to admit that in essence she is right; what she calls 'bringin' him up above his fortin' is impractical, and Mrs Glegg is a very practical woman, lending out money to her kin at interest, and questioning Tom closely about the investment she allows herself to make in his trading transactions. Her relationship with Mr Glegg is described with superb irony – one sees him seeking refuge in his garden, reading his wife's mood at the breakfast table, having sufficient spirit to skirmish with her and reaping the whirlwind of her tongue knowing, after that, that she will retire to her room with Baxter's 'Saints' Everlasting Rest'. She is excitable and quarrelsome, as Mrs Tulliver knows, but a period of self-inflicted meditation generally sees her repentance (though only to herself) of her earlier mood. In one instance she demonstrates her remarkable independence – she stands by Maggie, will not hear of her being condemned, and regards Stephen's letter as a proof of her innocence, which indeed it is. Here she is not influenced by public opinion; her life and habits are well-ordered, but she is no slave to convention. Aunt Glegg contributes much to the quality of the humour present in the Dodson sequences; her comments are never dull, in fact they are sometimes pertinent and impertinent. Mrs Glegg is childless, and George Eliot's presentation of her is psychologically penetrating; in a curious way she has something in common with Maggie, for she is an alert and intelligent woman with little outlet for her energies and abilities beyond the petty round of gossip, family affairs and material possessions.

Other Tulliver relations

I have given Aunt Glegg space to herself because her independent character deserves it. Her sisters, *Mrs Deane* and *Mrs Pullet*, merit some comment. The first is comparatively unimportant, though it is interesting to note that she has, unexpectedly, made the best marriage in terms of possessions and money, since her husband has risen to an important position with Guest and Company. She creates an unfortunate impression at the family meeting to discuss Tulliver's bankruptcy, being willing to buy only some of her sister's best possessions, nothing else being quite good enough for her. She is the mother of Lucy, but dies when the latter is seventeen. Mrs Pullet is much more clearly defined; elsewhere I have described her tearful hypochondria, but perhaps it would be as well to indicate that she is so obsessed by illness that she takes a morbid interest in death and disease in anyone local, sometimes identifying with it herself, and always prepared to recount the details. She is usually near to tears, and these dribble without much provocation, any family incident or chance mention being sufficiently moving to require them. Her many possessions include a large wardrobe full of fashionable clothes; she fears burglars and is so houseproud that Tom and Maggie have to take great care where they tread: once Tom has to sit with a towel round his boots.

Maggie's 'disgrace' gives Mrs Pullet full opportunity to display her melancholy; she fears the scandal attaching to

Maggie will have contaminated her reputation and that her acquaintances will no longer wish to know her. Weeping is her resource and her consolation.

The husbands of the three Dodson sisters are individually characterized, men who have made their way not merely into the family but also into the solidity of respectable middle-class achievement. *Mr Glegg* is perhaps the most sympathetically drawn. We are told that he is mean, and yet it is obvious that he has endearing qualities. He is kind-hearted for the most part, though he feels so sorry for Lucy that he is harsh towards Maggie. He has learned to accept his wife for what she is, and finds solace and fulfilment in his garden. But he has a delightful tendency to be facetious on his wife's account, and is not above provoking her a little. At the same time, he does not like to see her 'at variance with others', since he knows that her being so will interfere with his peace of mind.

Mr Pullet is much more of a caricature, regarded as something of a fool by Maggie and Tom, not an unfair judgement when one considers how little he contributes to conversation; he has made his way in the world, but shows no evidence of acumen above the ordinary. He appears to measure out his life in lozenges and peppermints, his musical snuff-box being more of an attraction than he is. Money rouses his attention — the thought of getting it and the thought of holding it — and at the family gathering he wants to know how much was loaned to Moss by Tulliver.

Mr Deane registers strongly with us on two occasions in the novel: the first, when Tom goes to him to apply for a position, and the second when, impressed by Tom's achievement in the firm, he offers him a share in it. He scorns Tom's education, largely because he is himself a self-made man, but gives him the opportunity to show his mettle. He considers buying back the Mill on one occasion so that Mr Tulliver can be put in, but does not contest Wakem's determination to acquire it. He is greatly influenced by his daughter Lucy, who is very fond of Maggie, and he sees to it that all the creditors are summoned to the dinner at which Tom is to settle his father's debts. Although he is hard on Maggie (understandably so, since he is witness to his daughter's anguish), he reveals the contents of Stephen's letter and provides Mrs Tulliver with a home as a housekeeper.

Lucy Deane is the natural contrast to Maggie; she is fair-haired, a true Dodson in appearance, well-behaved, clean, shy, speaking when she is spoken to; Maggie likes her, but on one occasion mentioned earlier in this account, becomes jealous of Tom's preference for her and pushes her into the mud. We are told that Lucy and Maggie go to boarding-school together, but after Mr Tulliver's downfall their ways diverge, for Maggie goes out to work as a governess, while Lucy, whose mother dies when she is seventeen, lives the life of a young girl of leisure in a small, but rather superior, St Ogg's society. To her credit, Lucy is not spoilt; she is kind to Mrs Tulliver, very fond of Maggie, and does her best to promote a match between Philip and Maggie, since she knows that the former is in love with her cousin. At the same time she is guileless, having no idea that Stephen, who has paid court to her, has fallen in love with Maggie, though the sharp sensitivity of Philip has seen this clearly. Meanwhile she also tries to get Philip to persuade his father to sell the Mill so that Tom can get it back into the family. Although it must be owned that she lacks the colour and overall interest of Maggie, she is capable of truly generous impulse, as she shows when she goes to Maggie to tell her not only that she forgives her, but also that she understands Maggie's own suffering in relation to Stephen. Lucy is affectionate and gentle, but beneath her somewhat placid exterior there is a capacity for suffering and a genuine concern for others.

Aunt Gritty is the last of the relations to be described: Mr Tulliver's much-loved sister who has come down in the world since she married the 'buck of Basset', the improvident Mr Moss. She is very like Maggie in the warmth and impetuosity of her feelings, and like her brother too, but she has learned patience through poverty; she is 'prolific', but her large family is testimony to her loving heart. In relation to her brother she stands as Maggie to Tom, but although she is worn out by the struggle to exist, her sincerity shines through her every action.

One of her poor children, who is a pale reflection of Maggie, sends to that superior cousin an egg; when her brother is disgraced, Gritty arrives unheralded – the poor relation with a heart among the rich relations who lack simple generosity – and we know that she would do anything to repay the money to her brother. Ironically, her hour of need is his, but the stricken Tulliver does not fail her – as Tom is to fail Maggie – for he cancels her debt. Maggie loves her very much, and goes to stay with her until Stephen comes in search of her.

Stephen Guest

He might have been sitting for his portrait, which would have represented a rather striking young man of five-and-twenty . . . (VI, i)

Stephen cannot be the hero of *The Mill on the Floss*, since we do not meet him until the opening of Book Sixth, and in any case his attributes are hardly heroic, if we except his appearance referred to above. He has paid court to Lucy and is thought to be engaged to her; he is elegant, indolent, somewhat sarcastic and trivial (witness the tormenting of Minny with the scissors when we first see him), but critics who have dismissed him do him some injustice. Before he meets Maggie he mocks her, but realizes when he sees her that she is unlike any other woman of his acquaintance or experience. He is courteous and considerate to her, and these qualities represent a sensitivity and awareness which those who refer to him as 'vulgar' have missed. Admittedly, references to his 'attar of roses' and the stress on his appearance and manners tend to create an impression of superficiality, but we must remember that to Maggie he is a person from another area of society, an area with which she is not familiar. Stephen has a fine voice, and it is through this voice that his feelings speak out to Maggie. Stephen realizes depths in his own feelings that he did not know existed before he met Maggie. He has been content to make sarcastic rejoinders, teasing remarks to Lucy, thinking himself in love in rather a patronizing way; but Maggie rouses him sexually – witness his kissing of her arm in the conservatory or their meeting in the lane at Aunt Gritty's – and challenges him mentally and emotionally. One senses always the temperature of his reactions – the meaningful looks, the contrived meetings, the confession and the guilt – the whole process of finding yourself in love when you did not wish to be in love. The psychological preparation for Stephen's effect upon Maggie has been called inadequate, but there is no psychological preparation for the suddenness of falling in love. Stephen is the great temptation, and he suffers the greatness of that temptation too. He drifts with Maggie on a current far stronger than that of the river, the current of passionate emotion which only the years of separation can finally still. He is broken by Maggie's wish to return and above all by her leaving him in Mudport, but he has the character to give the true account of their 'elopement' and to exonerate her from all blame. His impassioned letter urging her still to join him, despite the wrong he knows they will do to others, has been called selfish and shallow. To this writer it is a letter from the heart, real because immediately felt; George Eliot defended Stephen from the strictures of the critics, for she knew that the power of sudden feeling for another changes lives, situations, conventions, so that the basis of ordered life falls away, as in a flood.

Philip Wakem

. . . this melancholy boy's face; the brown hair round it waved and curled at the ends like a girl's. (II, iii)

Philip's hump back occurred in childhood, and the result was to make him hypersensitive physically and socially. We first meet him in the schoolroom at Stelling's, where his ability to draw animals and to tell stories impresses Tom, who has been conditioned to dislike him because of his father's hatred of Wakem. Driven back upon himself by his disability, Philip compensates by intensive study and artistic ability; he has little in common with Tom, but when Maggie comes on a visit he finds a kinship of sensitivity and interest. He forms a strong attachment to her, and on one occasion makes a sketch of her which he shows her years later. His concern that Tom shall not suffer as he, Philip, has suffered, is shown when he gets permission from Mr Stelling to tell Tom that he will suffer no permanent injury as a result of the accident with Mr Poulter's sword. This considerateness wins him Maggie's affection, and she grows fond of him, knowing that he values her more than Tom does. Years later they meet and form a close friendship which on Philip's side is love; he is morbid and sensitive though, and deep down he knows that Maggie's love is born of compassion and affection rather than the love he craves. He deplores Maggie's discovery of Thomas à Kempis, considering that renunciation of self means the destruction of the full nature which she possesses, which should be outward-going and loving, not sterile. He is interested in art and literature and music, and is able to provide the culturally-starved Maggie with means of sustenance. She is committed to him, but when Tom learns of their meetings he confronts Philip with Maggie in the Red Deeps and forces them to break it off. Maggie is disgusted and humiliated, Philip's morbid sensitivity is driven to breaking-point, but they are to meet again at Lucy Deane's.

When they do Philip is prepared to keep Maggie out of trouble by merely acknowledging her, but Maggie's warmth – and Tom patronizingly does not mind them meeting in the company of others – awakes his old feelings, and these are heightened when he realizes that Stephen loves Maggie, and he also suspects that that love is returned. From them on he suffers acutely and, ironically, is instrumental in placing temptation in their way on that fatal morning when they drift with the current. His fine sensitivity is bruised, but he will hear no evil of Maggie, and his letter to her shows that in loving her he has experienced a fulfilment denied to him in any other experience of his life.

Mr Wakem

'I shall have no direct transactions with young Tulliver.' (VI, viii)

Wakem is slandered by Mr Tulliver, for he has acted on behalf of Pivart, who wins his case against the Mill-owner. We meet Wakem only four times in the narrative, and do not find him unsympathetic on the whole. There is every reason for his contempt of Tulliver, and his courteous turning away of Mrs Tulliver when she comes to see him can be explained quite simply by the fact that he knows he has been abused. He acts from immediate rancour, buys the Mill, and puts Tulliver in as manager, thus being revenged for the curses heaped on him. So far we do not feel drawn towards him, but there is little animosity of a personal nature in him until the terrible incident when he is half-flogged to death, as he puts it, by Tulliver before his final stroke. Imagine his reaction when he learns from Philip later that he, Philip, loves Maggie! Wakem proves to have considerable feeling for Philip and, after snarling and objecting, comes round to Philip's point of view and makes himself known to Maggie at the bazaar. In addition he lets the Mill go back into the Tulliver family, for Tom takes it over when it is purchased by Guest and Company after the joint manoeuvring of Lucy and Philip. His great redeeming feature is his love of his deformed son, to whom he is indulgent, kind and tolerant – in fact, a good father.

Bob Jakin

Bob Jakin, originally employed to scare the birds away from the corn, is one of Tom's companions until their quarrel over Bob's cheating. He is sharp, interested in country sports (like rat-catching with ferrets), and as he gets older his abilities are concentrated on making money and doing a little trading on the side for himself. He throws away the knife that Tom gave him, but retrieves it, doubtless with a view to realizing its value later. But he does not forget, and when Mr Tulliver is made bankrupt Bob comes to the house and offers Tom nine sovereigns in return for that gift of long ago, the only present he had ever received. This is typical of Bob, who has a kind heart and is always prepared to act kindly towards those he values, like Maggie and Tom. He demonstrates this in two ways: he buys books for Maggie, for he has heard her bemoaning the fact that hers have gone in the selling-up and, secondly, he puts Tom in the way of making some money from private trading which ultimately leads to the paying off of Mr Tulliver's creditors. He provides Tom with a lodging when he works in St Ogg's, is very conscious of his lower rank as a pedlar, shows how persuasive he can be when he gets Aunt Glegg interested in putting money into Tom's trading venture, and shelters Maggie when she returns to St Ogg's after the drifting with Stephen. By this time he is married, but he always treats Maggie with a natural deference, threatens anyone who speaks evil of her, even helps her to free the boat in which she sets off to try to rescue Tom. He is generous and sly (perhaps all his money isn't made honestly), a thoroughly likeable and convincing character. He represents George Eliot's faith in simple, unpretentious human nature.

Narrative art and style

The Mill on the Floss is rich in texture and patterning; from the opening sequence, where the author imagines herself dreaming with her arms resting on a stone bridge, George Eliot's own voice controls and shapes the action of the novel. The presence of the author in the narrative – of the teller in the tale – is a favourite device of nineteenth-century fiction; it is employed, for example, by Dickens and Thackeray, who in turn inherited it from Fielding, Smollett and Sterne. The great precursors of the mid nineteenth-century novelists, Scott and Jane Austen, also use the omniscient tone, frequently interrupting the story proper in order to comment on character, situation, dilemma or decision, or even to establish historical or geographical setting. In *The Mill on the Floss* the tradition is maintained and even extended; the first chapter, like the last, has the presence of the author as confiding agent:

As I look at the full stream . . . I am in love with moistness . . . I have been pressing my elbows on the arms of my chair . . .

A friendly intimacy with the reader is at once established, and the result is an ethos at once sympathetic and warm, entirely appropriate to a narrative which is to be concerned with an investigation of human nature.

Sometimes the author's voice is less intimate than here; sometimes it is informed with a vast learning, with philosophical speculation, with indicating analogies between the Tullivers and their tribulations and a wider life. Book Fourth ('The Valley of Humiliation') opens with just such an authorial sequence. Here the tone is prophetic as well, linking the Floss with a much more important river:

Journeying down the Rhone on a summer's day, you have perhaps felt the sunshine made dreary by those ruined villages which stud the banks in certain parts of its course, telling how the swift river once rose, like an angry, destroying god, sweeping down the feeble generations whose breath is in their nostrils, and making their dwellings a desolation. (IV, i)

This anticipates the climax of the novel, and the further implication is that the river is to be equated with the river of life, the destiny of the characters who live by it, and, of course, Tom and Maggie in particular. Here the whole chapter is an author comment, but generally George Eliot's interventions are much briefer; they are moral, ironic, learned, philosophical, witty. Generally speaking, they provide *The Mill on the Floss* with a type of authenticity – the feel of wisdom, of human and spiritual knowledge, so that the reader senses the essential truth of the author's authority, that the life she describes is related to her own life experience expresses imaginatively, intellectually and, above all, humanly. As you, the reader, follow out the story of *The Mill on the Floss*, pay close attention to the author's voice and variants, for often George Eliot embodies in her own appraisal a considered comment on an aspect of the human condition.

Sometimes the author uses her voice to convey historical perspective, and in the section on 'Background and chronology' I have indicated specific reference to actual events, and these are also in the textual notes to the chapters. In addition to the factual, however, George Eliot creates a mythology for St Ogg's which gives to the story of Maggie Tulliver a particular poignancy. We remember that she tells us how Ogg the son of Beorl rowed the woman in rags across the Floss; she is transformed 'into robes of flowing white, and her face became bright with exceeding beauty, and there was a glory around it' (I, xii). The legend becomes part of the history of the town, and 'Ogg the son of Beorl was always seen with his boat upon the wide-spreading waters, and the Blessed Virgin sat in the prow, shedding a light around as of the moon in its brightness, so that the rowers in the gathering darkness took heart and pulled anew' (I, xii). There follows a potted history of St Ogg's (in the author's voice), with more than a glance at religious controversy through the ages, and the result is that almost by subliminal association the position of Maggie (the Virgin of St Ogg's) and the public discussion of her (moral controversy) becomes part of the *continuing* history of the town. The effect is that the author has succeeded in providing not merely a physical setting but a moral and spiritual one, too, thus extending the dimensions and associations of her story.

We feel, too, that George Eliot has one area upon which she dwells with loving care, and her voice is used but this time obliquely rather than first person direct. The town of St Ogg's is Gainsborough, but the countryside described with such affection is surely the Warwickshire of the author's childhood. Natural description runs throughout the novel and the commonplace expression of it, as distinct from the lyrical, extends to the chapter headings: for example, 'The Torn Nest is Pierced by the Thorns'. The early part of *The Mill on the Floss* has much fine description to commend it, while the sequences in the Red Deeps are enhanced by a lyrical and sometimes spiritual quality. Here is an early description, redolent of nostalgia, calling forth 'thoughts that do often lie too deep for tears':

These familiar flowers, these well-remembered bird-notes, this sky with its fitful brightness, these furrowed and grassy fields, with a sort of personality given to it by the capricious hedgerows – such things as these are the mother tongue of our imagination, the language that is laden with all the subtle inextricable associations the fleeting hours of our childhood left behind them. (I, v)

By the time Maggie comes to meet Philip in the Red Deeps the tone has changed, as befits the mood required. She is unaware of his presence, and is intent on contemplating the delights of nature in which she finds herself:

She was calmly enjoying the free air, while she looked up at the old fir trees, and thought that those broken ends of branches were the record of past storms, which had only made the red stems soar higher. (V, i)

This emphasizes the narrowness of Maggie's constriction – nature is her only freedom – and it is fitting that her friendship with Philip, which extends that freedom by embracing the mutual appreciation of the cultural, artistic and literary, should be set against the background of nature. It is no accident that much of the imagery which particularizes Maggie associates her directly with nature ('With her dark colouring and jet crown surmounting her tall figure, she seems to have a sort of kinship with the grand Scotch firs'), and it may be added that both *Adam Bede* and *Silas Marner* have title-page quotations from Wordsworth, the poet of nature much admired by George Eliot, who would surely have endorsed those sublime lines from *Tintern Abbey* (1798):

> For I have learned
> To look on nature, not as in the hour
> Of thoughtless youth; but hearing oftentimes
> The still, sad music of humanity

Nature is at the heart of *The Mill on the Floss*, giving to the childhood of Tom and Maggie what George Eliot was later to call in *Daniel Deronda* 'the love of tender kinship for the face of earth': it is the record of change, or rather the background to it, for just as the seasons change so changes the heart of man or, in this case, woman as epitomized by Maggie Tulliver.

The unifying factual and symbolic use of water in the form of the river itself gives *The Mill on the Floss* an allegorical as well as a specific meaning. As I have said, it is the river of life, fate or destiny, the onward movements and effects which make history. It is part of George Eliot's narrative art that from the first chapter onwards we are never allowed to forget the river and its influence, and immediately the associations or suggestions are heightened by the nature of the language. George Eliot speaks of 'the loving tide . . . checks its passage with an impetuous embrace', and when we have read the novel and thought back to that phrase we are reminded inevitably of Maggie; later on the same page (I, i) we are told that the Floss 'seems to me like a living companion while I wander along the bank and listen to its low placid voice, as to the voice of one who is deaf and loving'. Here the simple personification conveys the trust and love of what is known as daily experience, but the writing is imbued again with the irony of change – the tranquillity which becomes a tempest in the last chapter of the novel. The personification also adds to the effect by making the river a living force, something that goes on beyond the destiny of man. Even in asides, like Mrs Tulliver's fears that Maggie will some day fall in the water and be drowned, the river is omnipresent, and just as in the first description the 'rush of the water, and the booming of the mill, bring a dreamy deafness', so in a later sequence on the river Maggie seems to drift as in a dream into the compromising commitment to Stephen. When they are on the Dutch vessel Maggie has a real dream, and here George Eliot uses the legend, the present, and the symbol of the river to define the nature of Maggie's guilt:

. . . She was in a boat on the wider water with Stephen, and in the gathering darkness something like a star appeared, that grew and grew till they saw it was the Virgin seated in St Ogg's boat, and it came nearer and nearer, till they saw the Virgin was Lucy and the boatman was Philip – no, not Philip, but her brother, who rowed past without looking at her; and she rose to stretch out her arms and call to him, and their own boat turned over with the movement, and they began to sink, till with one spasm of dread she seemed to awake, and find she was a child again in the parlour at evening twilight, and Tom was not really angry. (VI, xiv)

This underlines a main facet of George Eliot's narrative art – her ability to give unity to her novel, to bring the various strands of the plot together, to make sure that everything within the book contributes to what Henry James, I think, called 'total relevance'. If you look at the above quotation you will see the associations of guilt and wish-fulfilment, the past and the present, and even an anticipation of the climax when the boat turns over. Maggie longs for reconciliation, and the 'and Tom was not really angry' shows the depth of that wish.

These, then – the use of her own voice in various ways, the presentation of nature as image and symbol, the emphasis on the river as the central symbol at once of life and death, destiny and fulfilment – are the main aspects of George Eliot's narrative art. Subserving them – and they will not be treated at the same length here – are those elements of style which give the narrative George Eliot's individual quality. Physical description, of places and of people, is the central stylistic device: thus St Ogg's is given its own personality, 'it's aged, fluted red roofs and the broad gables of its wharves', while each person who is to play a part in the tragic story which unfolds before us is physically portrayed. Mrs Tulliver is 'a blond comely woman, in a fan-shaped cap'; Maggie, according to her father, is a straight black-eyed wench as anybody need wish to see'. Mrs Glegg is described in great detail, even down to the 'fronts' which she chooses to wear for different occasions, but it is when we read the account of the appearance presented by the Pullets that we note the linking of physical description with simile and metaphor. The ironic tone is a fine one:

Mr Pullet was a small man with a high nose, small twinkling eyes, and thin lips, in a fresh-looking suit of black and a white cravat, that seemed to have been tied very tight on some higher principle than that of mere personal ease. He bore about the same relation to his tall, good-looking wife, with her balloon sleeves, abundant mantle, and large be-feathered and be-ribboned bonnet, as a small fishing-smack bears to a brig with all its sails spread. (I, vii)

Here the tone is humorous, the language a mixture of the plain and direct and the fanciful, almost a reflection of the couple themselves. It is obvious that physical description makes character visual and immediate, and in *The Mill on the Floss* the duality of character – what is seen and what goes on in the consciousness – is the main concern of the author. Maggie's consciousness is explored in depth, and in the section on 'Characters' I have indicated what George Eliot achieved in terms of the psychological integration of her characters.

But character is seen largely through speech, and George Eliot's style embraces faithful and convincing *dialogue* on the one hand and a superb and accurate rendering of *dialect* on the other. Consider the emotional temperature – momentary, yet felt – of the following exchange between Mr Tulliver and Mrs Glegg:

'If you talk o' that,' said Mr Tulliver, 'my family's as good as yours – and better, for it hasn't got a damned ill-tempered woman in it.'

'Well!' said Mrs Glegg, rising from her chair, 'I don't know whether you think it's a fine thing to sit by and hear me swore at, Mr Glegg; but I'm not going to stay a minute longer in this house. You can stay behind, and come home with the gig – and I'll walk home.' (I, vii)

Bob Jakin uses dialect ('I'd sooner be a rat-catcher nor anything – I would') as does Mr Tulliver; but in the Tullivers George Eliot strikes again that rich ore of proverbial language which characterized Mrs Poyser in *Adam Bede*. Mr Tulliver has a store of cliché-proverbs which he produces in I, iii, and if he does not utter them, George Eliot tells us what he 'often said'. Examples are: 'if you drive your waggon in a hurry, you may light on an awkward corner'; 'I'll niver pull my coat off before I go to bed'; 'I shan't be put off wi' spoon-meat afore I've lost my teeth'. All these add to the authenticity of the novel, making the speech-habits of the past living to the present.

It will be quite evident from the foregoing that one of the memorable aspects of *The Mill on the Floss* is the quality of the humour. George Eliot has an understanding not only of the simple rustic mind (as she was to show in the Rainbow Inn scene in *Silas Marner*) but also of the slow-thinking and the sharp. Sometimes this is allied to pathos in *The Mill on the Floss*, for example where Mrs Tulliver is bemoaning the loss of her possessions after the sale at the Mill. The humour is obviously present in the author's voice, for although she deplores Mrs Tulliver's small worldliness, a different inflection is heard when she describes Bob Jakin's superb countering of Mrs Glegg's patronage. The motivation behind Bob is to get

Mrs Glegg to put up the money for Tom's private trading, with, of course, some profit to herself. The method is consistent self-demeaning:

'No, mum. I know my place,' said Bob, lifting up his pack and shouldering it. 'I'm not going t'expose the lowness o' my trade to a lady like you. Packs is come down i' the world: it 'ud cut you to th' heart to see the difference . . .' (V, ii)

Consider, too, the humour inherent in the description of Aunt Pullet, as she 'sent the muscles of her face in quest of fresh tears as she advanced into the parlour', and later, 'but Mrs Pullet had married a gentleman farmer, and had leisure and money to carry her crying and everything else to the highest pitch of respectability' (I, vii). The humour of *The Mill on the Floss*, then, is proverbial, pathetic, ironic, sometimes with a fine coating of innuendo, sometimes with an overall wise appraisal of the slow-witted or the cunning, as the case may be. There is an easy mastery, a fine facility of expression, a truthful identification with sound and sense.

George Eliot is the master of narrative tension, or suspense, bringing graphic immediacy to the story in terms of situation. *The Mill on the Floss* alternates between small and large crises throughout the length of its action: Maggie cutting off her hair, Maggie pushing Lucy into the mud and then running away to the gipsies, Tom being injured by the sword, Mr Tulliver's first stroke, the execution of the bill of sale – all these are the stuff of dramatic narration. The reader is never far from the edge of tension, and as the plot unfolds the emotional crises become more fraught with implications: Tulliver's flogging of Wakem, Maggie's drifting with Stephen, Maggie's return to Tom and his rejection of her, and finally, of course, the tremendous impact of the flood, where the story flows like the river and is at one with it. Perhaps this ability to keep the reader *with* the characters, in sympathy and in action, is the salient feature of George Eliot's style; it reflects her attention to the *emotional* temperature of the novel, and we may say that a limpid style attends the action when the barometer is set fair, a heavier and more deliberate tone when change is imminent. And we must add to this a facility of poetic expression which is always there; metaphors and similes abound from a wide range of reference – natural, literary, artistic, learned, spiritual. Maggie in youth is compared to a Skye terrier and as a young woman to a tall Hamadryad. Frederick Harrison observed of another fine novel by George Eliot, *Felix Holt*, that one had to read it with the same attention to detail as one would give to a poem like Tennyson's *In Memoriam*. Harrison was not thinking merely of the poetic quality of the novel, but of the learning, wisdom and humanity which formed the main stitches in its fabric. Read *The Mill on the Floss* for what it can tell you of life: the life of man and woman, boy and girl, and the life of the imagination implicit in its language.

General questions and sample answer in note form

General questions

1 'George Eliot shows a wonderful understanding of the mind of a child.' Discuss this statement.

2 What are the merits of *The Mill on the Floss* as a novel?

3 'The Victorian novel was long because the people of the nineteenth century wanted it so.' Do you think that it is *too* long? Give reasons for your answer.

4 It has been said that the first part of *The Mill on the Floss* is so much longer than the second part that the end of the story seems unreal. Do you agree with this?

5 How far did Tom try to carry out his father's dying request, and how far did he succeed?

6 The later part of the book has been described as melodrama. Do you think that this is a true criticism?

7 What is the importance to the plot of (a) the sword lent to Tom by Mr Poulter, and (b) Mrs Kenn's illness at the time of the bazaar?

8 On what occasions did Maggie come into contact with Lawyer Wakem? What were the results of these meetings?

9 Show how the beginning and the end of the book are linked carefully together.

10 How did Maggie first meet Philip Wakem? What lasting effect had this meeting upon her?

11 What episodes in the story do you think reveal (a) suspense, (b) humour, (c) pathos?

12 What do you learn from this book of the Victorian attitude to women?

13 Would you like to have lived in St Ogg's? What is your opinion of the polite society of that town?

14 What part is played in the story by the River Floss?

15 Write an essay on George Eliot's use of humour in *The Mill on the Floss*.

16 How far does Maggie's own character bring her into trouble, and how far is she the victim of circumstances?

17 What do we learn about the character of Tom Tulliver by the way in which he treats his father, his sister, Philip Wakem?

18 How does Mr Tulliver's family differ from Mrs Tulliver's? Explain the differences in detail.

19 Write character-sketches of two of Mrs Tulliver's sisters.

20 What is your opinion of Lucy Deane? Do you think that George Eliot's description of her is true to life?

21 What does the quarrel between Mr Wakem and Mr Tulliver tell you about the lawyer? Do you think that he was right to act as he did?

22 What opinions about Philip Wakem are expressed by (a) Mr Deane, (b) Mr Tulliver, (c) Aunt Pullet?

23 Philip Wakem's deformity makes him difficult to portray. Does George Eliot make her readers understand Maggie's feelings for him?

24 Stephen Guest does not appear until almost the end of the story. Do you think that he is made attractive to the reader?

25 'Although apparently a minor character, Bob Jakin appears at every crucial moment in the history of Tom and Maggie Tulliver.' Discuss this statement.

26 Critics have frequently referred to George Eliot's powers of characterization as 'masterly'. Do you agree with their judgement?

27 Discuss the good and the bad points of George Eliot's style with regard to the words and figures of speech she uses.

28 Write an appreciation of the humorous parts of the book.

29 Write a critical account of George Eliot's use of her own voice in the novel.

30 Write an essay on George Eliot's use of image and symbol in *The Mill on the Floss*.

Suggested notes for essay answer to question 1

(a) *Introduction* – brief summary of the childhood sequence of the novel in order to demonstrate how much of the action – slightly over half – is devoted to the examination of childhood.

(b) Concentrate first on Maggie, who is the central focus, but also apply the term 'a child' to Tom and, if you feel you know their characters well enough, to Lucy and Bob Jakin. Show how George Eliot understands the main facets of Maggie's character, and then after general statements proceed to indicate by close reference to the text what they are.

(c) George Eliot's understanding of Maggie's sensitivity – her dependence – her impetuosity – her love of her father – her overwhelming love for Tom – her jealousy (for example, of Lucy) – her need for the fetish – then go on to:

(d) Her happiness (pick two incidents), her misery as a result of her own shortcomings (forgetfulness over the rabbits) – her cleverness (both before and after Tom goes to Mr Stelling) – her independence of thought and feeling (contrast with her *emotional* dependence) – the changes in her nature as a result of the tragedy – her capacity for renunciation – her conflicts with Tom – the reasons for them – her suffering.

(e) *Conclusion* – quote and refer to particular incidents which reiterate what you have said above (mention Philip as child bringing out Maggie's latent interests and sensitivity). Show how George Eliot understands Maggie through her language as well as by her commentary.

It would be possible to demonstrate George Eliot's understanding of Tom's mind in the same way: you could refer to his healthy animal spirits, his sense of inheritance, his competition with Bob (and his social sense of superiority to him), his physicality (which accounts in part at least for his dislike of Philip) and so on.

Further reading

Other novels by George Eliot (readily available in Penguin Books and Oxford World's Classics), including:

Adam Bede (1859)
Silas Marner (1861)
Middlemarch (1871–2)

The standard biography is

George Eliot, by Gordon S. Haight (Oxford, 1968)

Other useful books are

A George Eliot Companion, F. B. Pinion (Macmillan, 1981)
The Mill on the Floss and Silas Marner, A Selection of Critical Essays, edited R. P. Draper, Casebook Series (Macmillan, 1977)
The Novels of George Eliot, Barbara Hardy (The Athlone Press, 1959)
George Eliot, Jennifer Uglow (Virago, 1987)

Brodie's Notes

TITLES IN THE SERIES

George Bernard Shaw	**Pygmalion**
Alan Sillitoe	**Selected Fiction**
John Steinbeck	**Of Mice and Men** and **The Pearl**
Alice Walker	**The Color Purple**

ENGLISH COURSEWORK BOOKS

Terri Apter	**Women and Society**
Kevin Dowling	**Drama and Poetry**
Philip Gooden	**Conflict**
Philip Gooden	**Science Fiction**
Margaret K. Gray	**Modern Drama**
Graham Handley	**Modern Poetry**
Graham Handley	**Prose**
Graham Handley	**Childhood and Adolescence**
R. J. Sims	**The Short Story**